IMAGES
of Rail

NEW YORK CENTRAL'S ST. LAWRENCE DIVISION 1940–1960

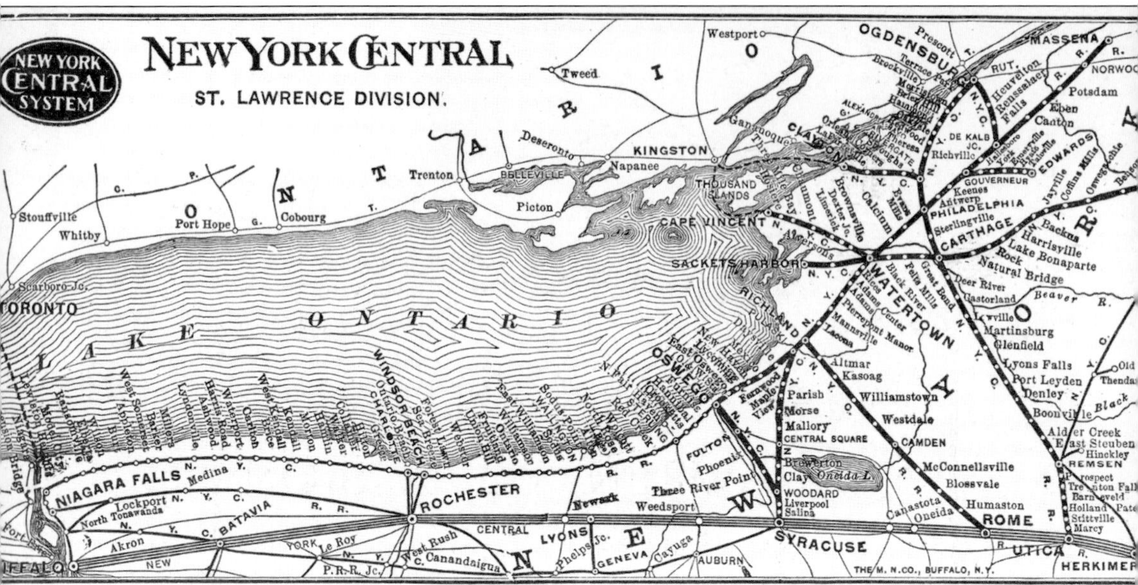

This pre-1940 map includes the later Rochester Division extending west from Oswego to the Suspension Bridge. Located north of Niagara Falls, the bridge connected the United States to Canada.

On the Cover: Seated in the fireman's seat and looking out the window is the author's longtime friend Jimmy Hart. An unidentified engineer stands in the gangway. A safety chain at his belt between the cab wall and tender was all the safety measure for not falling off the locomotive. This photograph was taken at Wilson, New York, in the mid-1930s. Research identifies the locomotive, which would soon be retired, as one of the fast passenger locomotives of that era. With only four high driving wheels, it was only good for short passenger train service, which was also diminishing rapidly.

IMAGES
of Rail

NEW YORK CENTRAL'S ST. LAWRENCE DIVISION 1940–1960

Allen Hilborn

ISBN 978-1-4671-0606-1

Published by Arcadia Publishing
Charleston, South Carolina

Printed in the United States of America

Library of Congress Control Number: 2021931854

For all general information, please contact Arcadia Publishing:
Telephone 843-853-2070
Fax 843-853-0044
E-mail sales@arcadiapublishing.com
For customer service and orders:
Toll-Free 1-888-313-2665

Visit us on the Internet at www.arcadiapublishing.com

This book is dedicated to the management and employees of the St. Lawrence Division, who gave me valuable insight into its operations. These people represented the finest in their professional crafts as well as offering great public relations. Their talent will never be duplicated.

Contents

ACKNOWLEDGMENTS

Preparation of this publication would have been difficult without the help and encouragement of many people and historical organizations. I will always be grateful. They are as follows: locomotive engineer Jimmy Hart, William Edson, Charles M. Smith, Lansing Vail, Richard Borsos, Lawrence A. Baggerly, the New York Central System Historical Society, Richard Stoving and the Edward May Photo Collection, Jefferson County Historical Society, and the *Watertown Daily Times*.

Unless otherwise noted, all images appear courtesy of the author's collection.

INTRODUCTION

It has always been my goal to outline one of the non-mainline divisions of the New York Central Railroad. Legendary and located in upstate New York, it contained more than 600 miles of track, including branches and running rights. It was an operating challenge and provided a productive bottom line for management. While the St. Lawrence Division has had relatively small attention in historical and rail-oriented publications, I have attempted to portray the periods of 1940 through 1960; this was the glory period of the greatest modern-day years of this 20th-century railroad legend. Very candid if not amusing details will be revealed to the reader. With no offense to the employees or the railroad, ingenuity often preceded the Book of Rules in getting the work done. This was especially true during mountainous snowfalls in the winter. Neighboring division crews had great respect for their "Hojack" colleagues, as the division was nicknamed. Officially, in 1940, the branch from West Yard in Oswego and continuing to the Suspension Bridge became part of the Rochester Division. Known as the "Red Line" because of its mostly seasonal fruit traffic and having been covered in other rail publications, no further discussion will be offered.

From the time I was a small child, trains have fascinated me. My formative years exposed me to the glamorous side of railroading as well as the quieter nondescript parts. My curiosity also caused me to wonder how these two extremes could come under the same railroad name. I also pondered if the attention of the higher powers was solely on the glamorous side?

This railroad I became acquainted with was the New York Central System. As a huge 10,000-mile railroad in the northeast, it stretched from New York City to Chicago and Boston to St. Louis. It was very easy for a railroad of this size to consume one's interest.

The mid-20th century was also a time of enormous change in the railroad industry. New technology affording economy, competition in transportation, reduced labor, and even politics were some of the factors.

My home at the time was in upstate New York, deep in the snow country when it was winter. The other three seasons were comfortable with typical northeast weather. Living in a small town that was on a branch line of the New York Central (NYC) gave me a whole different exposure to the railroad. While I have never heard this terminology used before, my town was on a branch line of a branch line. I was probably as distant from current trends of the railroad at the time.

There were two trains a day. One was a local passenger carrying mail and express on the headend. A coach and overnight Pullman from New York City brought up the rear. Carrying newspapers, it connected us with the world. The other train was a peddler freight arriving in the afternoon. Both of them were roundtrip affairs.

The local freight probably galvanized my interest in railroading. Being able to get up close to switching activities at the yard, one got a real feel of what railroading was like. What I would learn later were the techniques and moves going back to the early 20th century.

The crews were aware of my presence and were quite friendly. As I got to know them better, I found out the oldest member had a seniority date of 1910, with the youngest in the early 1920s. Working together was like watching a football team when switching freight cars.

Their public relations did not stop there. I would be given employee timetables, magazines, and even a NYC Book of Rules. Sometimes, these kindnesses would be left on the doorstep at home. Later on, when browsing through the rule book, I discovered how many rules were violated. As serious as it might seem, there was another rule to the effect "when in doubt, do the safest thing."

The other daily ritual with this crew came at the end of their switching before leaving town. Engine power in this day and time was steam. The locomotive was a small 10-wheeler perfect for the job. There was a water station opposite the depot for refreshing the engine. The engineer would get down from the cab, with his long spouted oil can, to lubricate the critical points of the valve gear and driving wheels. Another friendly man, he would walk over to greet me and focus his expertise on my bicycle chain.

When he learned I was related to one of his former freight customers, he offered an invite to the engine cab. For a young boy to suddenly experience an extra-hot cab temperature, the fragrance of soft coal burning, and hot grease from the moving parts, it was a different world. With the locomotive suddenly in motion, there was a rocking and swaying motion, plus catching an occasional cinder in my eye, but what an experience I would never forget. Harry Doonan was the consummate engineer and easily the man every red-blooded boy wanted to be.

A period of absence from upstate New York interrupted my usual railroad observer experiences. Returning a few years later, I was waiting at a crossing one afternoon when a diesel locomotive approached. Taking me by surprise, it stopped, with the engineer waving for me to come up in the cab. It turned out it was one of Doonan's firemen who recognized me. Little did I realize that this would be a turning point in my railroad experiences. Introductions were made to other enginemen, and conversations revealed many incidents opposite the romantic side of railroading.

Other opportunities awaited me in succeeding months and years. They included mainline divisions in central and western New York State. All of these men were familiar with the "Hojackers," as the St. Lawrence Division train people were referred to. These other "rocket" railroaders gave me a lot of smiles with their exhilarating speeds and gentle stops, without so much as a ripple in the water glass back in the dining car.

My heart, though, has always been with the St. Lawrence Division. Various times in the past half-century, I have dictated my writing about the various workings of the St. Lawrence Division, where its operation was reminiscent of the early 1900s. I must admit it was that good, so it did not need to be changed.

Unless one had been around the railroad and known the employees, the division has never had detailed information on the various lines and branches. Pictures have been difficult to find but granted, in my time, people did not find photography as conveniently as they can now.

To give this book as much credibility as possible, I have confined commentary and other material to the time period 1940–1960. The reason for these years is easily understandable. The railroad was physically intact, with no branches out of service. Various towns and cities had a great customer base. Steam power was still active, and passenger service still was available on half of the division.

The death knell fell in 1960 with division offices, including dispatching for both St. Lawrence and Adirondack, being moved to Utica, New York. Other eastern divisions were consolidated with the above to form the Eastern District. Things were moving toward a corporate merger and eventual disaster, which I will not comment on.

With the recent passing of several St. Lawrence men who were like fathers to me, I felt it more important than ever to complete this book with seniority names as well. Such a collection of personalities will never be duplicated. God bless them all!

One

St. Lawrence Division Physical Plant

As of 1940, former Rome, Watertown & Ogdensburg (RW&O) and, later, Ontario Division trackage from West Yard to the Niagara Falls Suspension Bridge became the Rochester Division. Labor agreements dating back to RW&O specified St. Lawrence train crews would operate over it. Running rights were also on two other railroads. The Rutland Railroad hosted St. Lawrence Division trains between Norwood and Malone, a distance of 37 miles.

The New York, Ontario & Western hosted division trains between Fulton and Oswego, a distance of 12 miles. There were reasons for a double track in those three areas. Leaving the Black River Valley at Watertown heading south, there was a considerable grade to Adams Center. In the steam era, helper locomotives were common. The second track allowed other trains to pass as the helpers returned to Watertown.

The Pulaski-to-Richland tracks were twofold. They handled East/West Oswego to Rome trains as well as the Syracuse/Massena traffic. It also facilitated opposing freight trains of considerable length. There were two reasons for the Oswego double track. Smoke in the tunnel could obscure another train unless it was on a designated track. Yard switching was extensive on both sides of the river, raising safety issues.

After the completion of the Massey Yard in Watertown, a new diesel house consisting of two tracks was built there. For the most part, just running repairs were performed. More extensive work was performed at DeWitt (Syracuse). While most locomotives on the division rotated through Utica or Dewitt at least once a week, the need for fueling and sand was done there.

Not previously mentioned were two specially equipped Alco S-4 switchers employing plug-in heaters on their engine blocks. These allowed engine shutdown during freezing weather. Their engine numbers were 8622 and 8623.

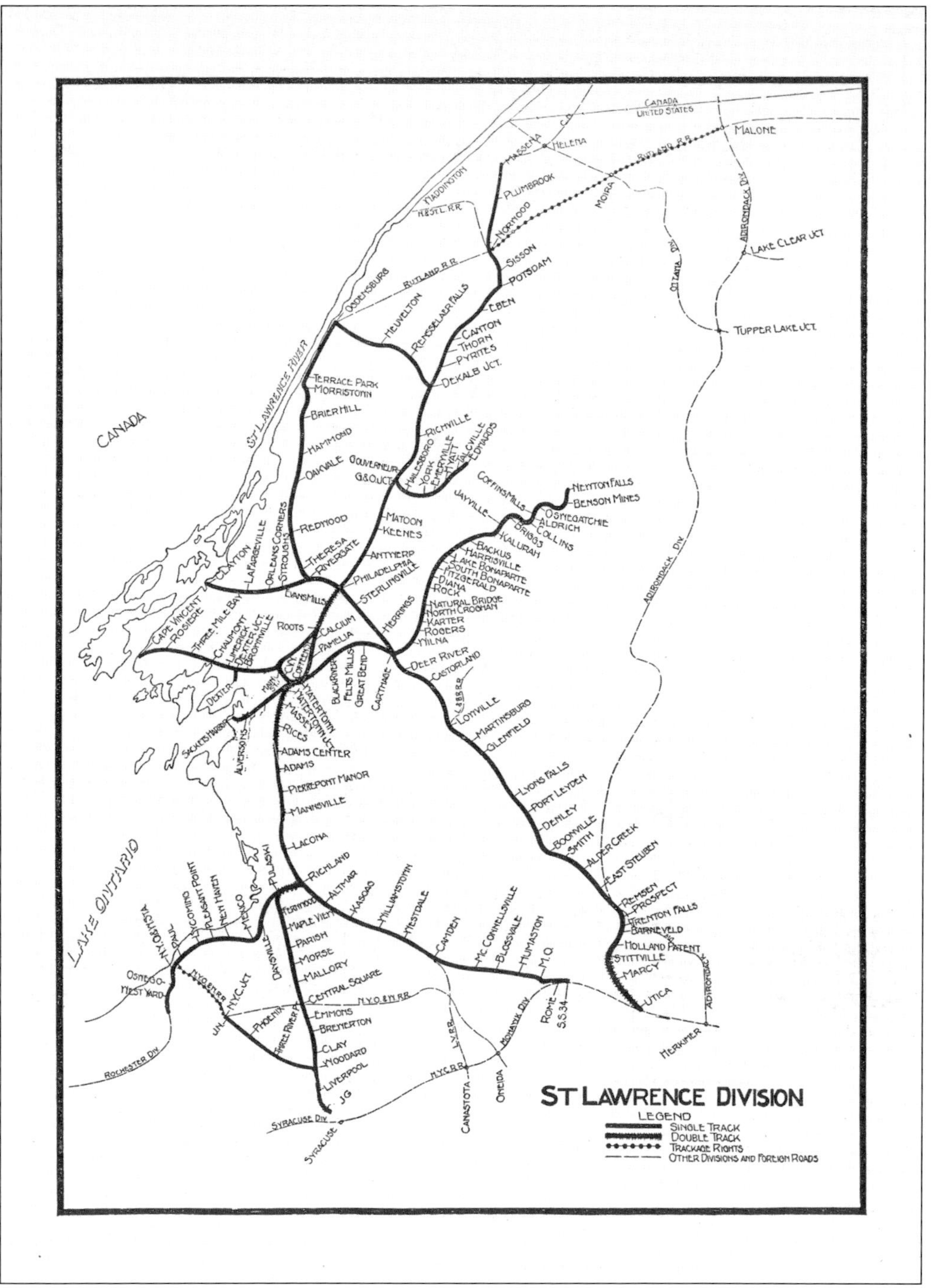

This is a map of the St. Lawrence Division tracks. Not showing on this map is the branch from Helena to Ottawa.

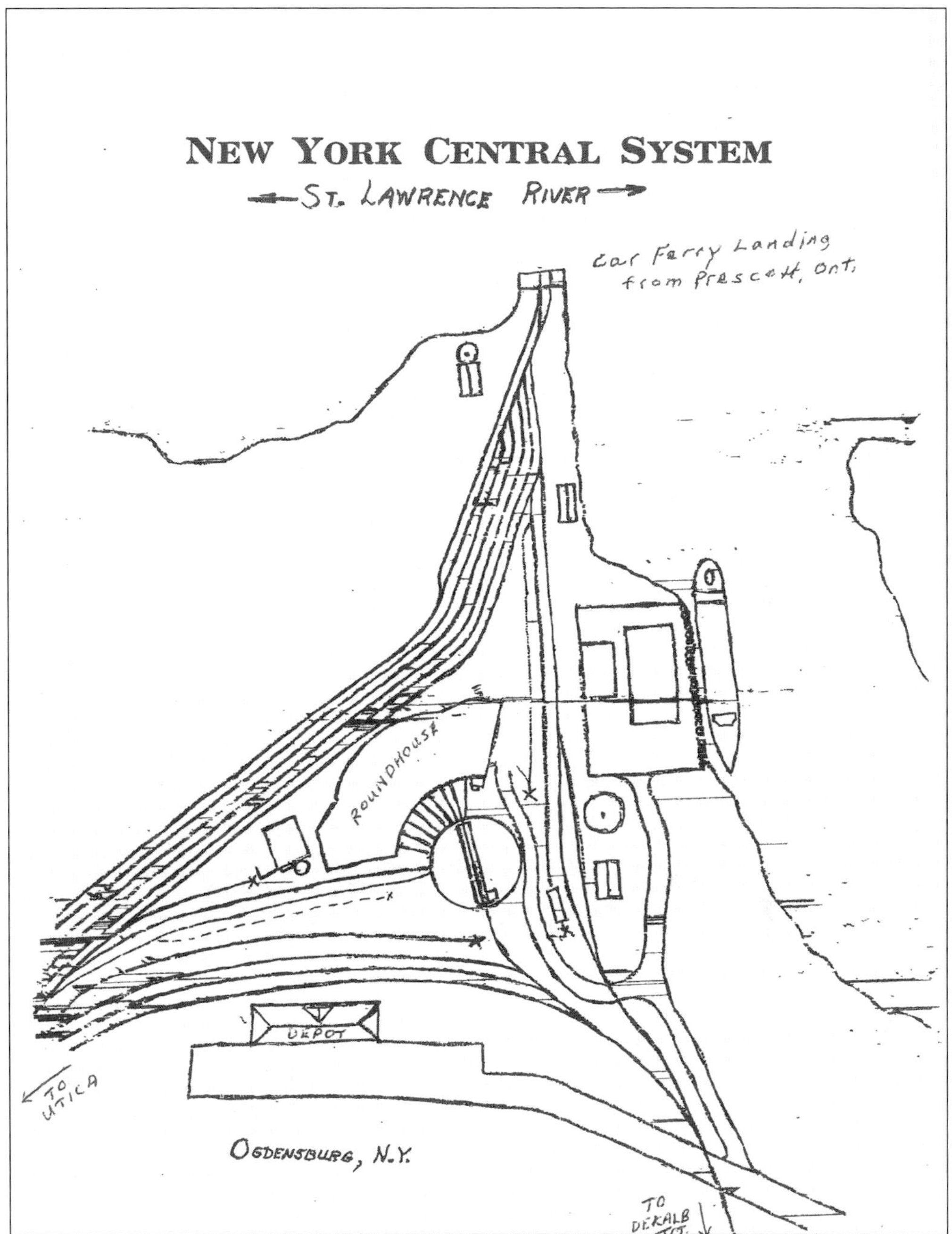

Shown here is a drawing of the New York Central System at the Ogdensburg, New York, depot. There was a car ferry landing from Prescott, Ontario.

This postcard view shows the trestle and rotating drawbridge spanning the bay at Chaumont, New York. Running 13.06 miles from Watertown, New York, this branch ran to Cape Vincent, New York. This location was responsible for engine and car restrictions on the line. The deteriorating condition restricted locomotives and cars of heavier axle weights reduced the branch back to Limerick in the early 1950s.

The only tunnel on the St. Lawrence Division is shown at East Bridge Street, Oswego, New York, in the 1950s. The position of the track proves that, at one time, there was a double track through the tunnel. The county courthouse is on the left, and the county office building is on the right of the tunnel in the photograph. The snowfall is mild compared to other times in the winter.

Just when one thought snow could not drift this high, a stalled NYC single-track snowplow is stranded in a 15-foot drift near Rosier, New York, as it makes its way toward Cape Vincent. The incident occurred on February 1, 1939. The smokestack of the pusher locomotive can barely be seen behind the plow. A rotary snowplow was later purchased and stationed at Watertown during the winter months. (Courtesy of the *Watertown Daily Times*.)

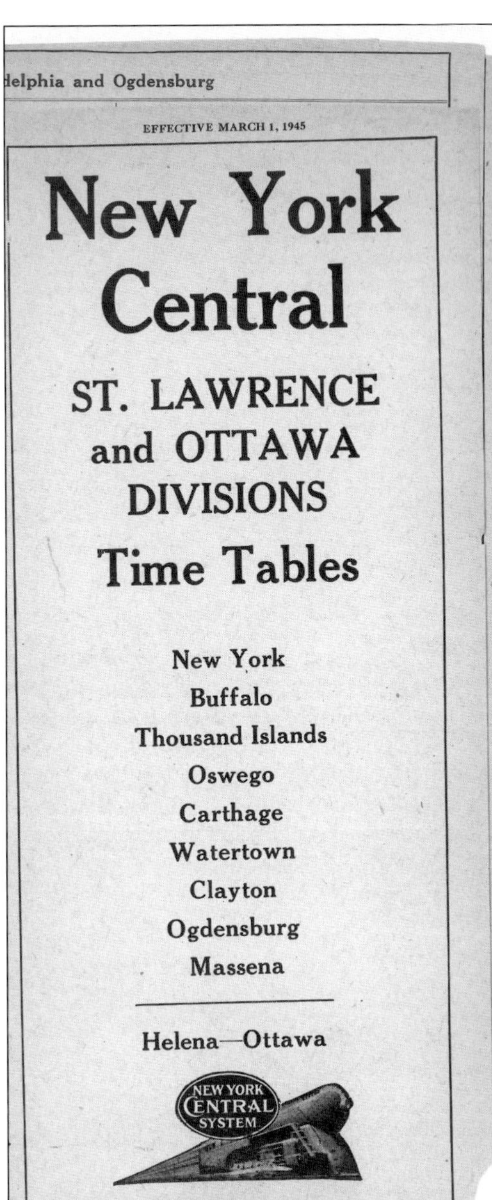
EFFECTIVE MARCH 1, 1945

New York Central

ST. LAWRENCE and OTTAWA DIVISIONS

Time Tables

New York
Buffalo
Thousand Islands
Oswego
Carthage
Watertown
Clayton
Ogdensburg
Massena

Helena—Ottawa

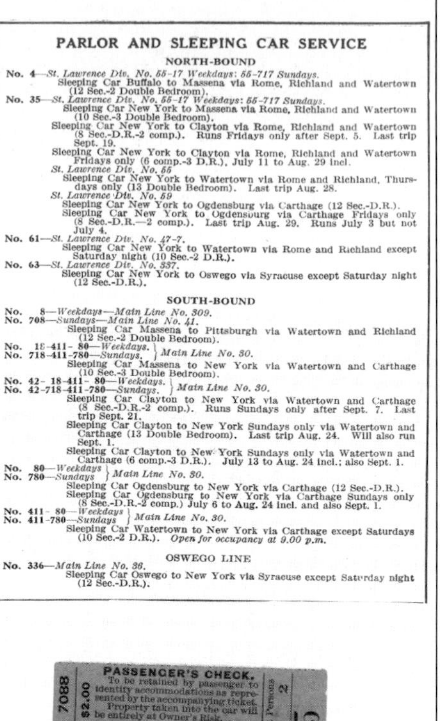

PARLOR AND SLEEPING CAR SERVICE

NORTH-BOUND

No. 4—*St. Lawrence Div. No. 55-17 Weekdays: 55-717 Sundays.*
Sleeping Car Buffalo to Massena via Rome, Richland and Watertown (12 Sec.-2 Double Bedroom).

No. 35—*St. Lawrence Div. No. 55-17 Weekdays: 55-717 Sundays.*
Sleeping Car New York to Massena via Rome, Richland and Watertown (10 Sec.-3 Double Bedroom).
Sleeping Car New York to Clayton via Rome, Richland and Watertown (8 Sec.-D.R.-2 comp.). Runs Fridays only after Sept. 5. Last trip Sept. 19.
Sleeping Car New York to Clayton via Rome, Richland and Watertown Fridays only (6 comp.-3 D.R.), July 11 to Aug. 29 incl.
St. Lawrence Div. No. 55
Sleeping Car New York to Watertown via Rome and Richland, Thursdays only (13 Double Bedroom). Last trip Aug. 28.
St. Lawrence Div. No. 59
Sleeping Car New York to Ogdensburg via Carthage (12 Sec.-D.R.).
Sleeping Car New York to Ogdensburg via Carthage Fridays only (8 Sec.-D.R.—2 comp.). Last trip Aug. 29. Runs July 3 but not July 4.

No. 61—*St. Lawrence Div. No. 47-7.*
Sleeping Car New York to Watertown via Rome and Richland except Saturday night (10 Sec.-2 D.R.).

No. 63—*St. Lawrence Div. No. 337.*
Sleeping Car New York to Oswego via Syracuse except Saturday night (12 Sec.-D.R.).

SOUTH-BOUND

No. 8—*Weekdays—Main Line No. 309.*
No. 708—*Sundays—Main Line No. 41.*
Sleeping Car Massena to Pittsburgh via Watertown and Richland (12 Sec.-2 Double Bedroom).

No. 18-411- 80—*Weekdays.* } *Main Line No. 30.*
No. 718-411-780—*Sundays.* }
Sleeping Car Massena to New York via Watertown and Carthage (10 Sec.-3 Double Bedroom).

No. 42- 18-411- 80—*Weekdays.* } *Main Line No. 30.*
No. 42-718-411-780—*Sundays.* }
Sleeping Car Clayton to New York via Watertown and Carthage (8 Sec.-D.R.-2 comp.). Runs Sundays only after Sept. 7. Last trip Sept. 21.
Sleeping Car Clayton to New York Sundays only via Watertown and Carthage (13 Double Bedroom). Last trip Aug. 24. Will also run Sept. 1.
Sleeping Car Clayton to New York Sundays only via Watertown and Carthage (6 comp.-3 D.R.). July 13 to Aug. 24 incl.; also Sept. 1.

No. 80—*Weekdays* } *Main Line No. 30.*
No. 780—*Sundays* }
Sleeping Car Ogdensburg to New York via Carthage (12 Sec.-D.R.).
Sleeping Car Ogdensburg to New York via Carthage Sundays only (8 Sec.-D.R.-2 comp.) July 6 to Aug. 24 incl. and also Sept. 1.

No. 411- 80—*Weekdays* } *Main Line No. 30.*
No. 411-780—*Sundays* }
Sleeping Car Watertown to New York via Carthage except Saturdays (10 Sec.-2 D.R.). *Open for occupancy at 9.00 p.m.*

OSWEGO LINE

No. 336—*Main Line No. 36.*
Sleeping Car Oswego to New York via Syracuse except Saturday night (12 Sec.-D.R.).

This time table is from March 1, 1945, and provides all the times and days for each train along the track.

Two

Steam Power

Unless one was a frequent observer of the Syracuse to Watertown main track, where larger steam power frequently operated, the St. Lawrence Division was home to a number of smaller-class engines. When it came to visual or audio drama, they could equal their larger brethren. The New York Central steam locomotives, regardless of age, were well-designed and frequently updated with the latest appliances to increase the efficiency of operation.

As the division had many branches with light rail and weight restrictions on bridges and trestles, low axle loadings were necessary. As it would turn out, the F-12e- and F-12g-class 10-wheeler would become the most versatile because of their ability to handle general-purpose work. As adaptable as they were, there were three branches that restricted them in 1940: Sacketts Harbor, Cape Vincent (beyond Chaumont), and the Newton Falls. This is where the smallest class E-1d would solve the problem. As the oldest steam power of this era, it still had the tractive effort to perform well.

As dieselization would cast a shadow on all steam power on the division in late 1951 and into 1952, all examples of the classes continued to run until the final curtain dropped.

The following classes were the most often seen depending on location. There were exceptions when mainline power was necessary for a high-tonnage train.

Class	Date Built	Wheel Arrangement	Weight	Boiler Pressure
B-10	1912	0-6-0	170,000	180
E-1	1899	2-6-0	155,200	190
F-12	1907	4-6-0	203,000	200
11-5	1912	2-8-2	274,000	180
11-6	1918	2-8-2	300,500	200
K-3	1912	4-6-2	272,000	200
K-11	1910	4-6-2	266,000	200
U-2	1912	0-8-0	218,000	180
U-3	1913	0-8-0	219,500	175

E-1d class NYC 2-6-0 mogul 1926 is shown in Watertown, New York. With smokestack capped, it appears out of service despite the relatively good appearance. Records reveal the locomotive was scrapped in November 1950.

The E-1d 1919 at Watertown, New York, on August 27, 1950, represents another example of the E-class engines. The slide-valve cylinders define them as the oldest motive power remaining on the railroad. Their build date of November 1899 gave them 51 years of service. (Stoving/May collection.)

The F-12 class represented the backbone of the motive power division. Here is the F-12e 834 at Utica, New York, on May 17, 1940. The engine was later renumbered to 1247. It has received a larger tender and is also carrying an ATS (automatic train stop) shoe on tender for mainline running between Utica and Rome. (Stoving/May collection.)

An F-12e 1249 is pictured at Utica, New York, on October 15, 1950. This was another engine with the ATS device, a safety measure for high speeds on mainline tracks. Non-ATS engines were restricted to lower speeds. (Stoving/May collection.)

F-12e 1251 is shown in DeWitt, New York, on July 15, 1948. Bright sunlight reveals the details of the engine. F-12s had high cabs for smaller engines. The engines had a tendency to weave at lower speeds but were straight as an arrow as speed increased.

F-12e 1254 is shown opposite roundhouse at East Syracuse, New York, On July 17, 1948. An occasional visitor on ST-5/6, it served as the local freight power from DeWitt to Fulton, New York, when regular engine 1279 was having a monthly inspection.

F-12e 1257 is in front of the roundhouse in Utica on July 16, 1949. The engineer in the cab window provides a reference for the height of the cab, about 12 feet above the rail. (Author's collection.)

F-12g 1262 is pictured at DeWitt, New York, on September 15, 1949. This photogenic crew wanted to be noticed in the picture. This was the regular engine powering 336/337 Syracuse to Oswego passenger local for a period of time. (Author's collection.)

With the Oswego, New York, enginehouse in the background, F-12g 850 is shown waiting for service. This engine was later renumbered to 1263. With no trailing truck behind the drivers of the F-12s, the third set of drivers were irregularly spaced to improve weight distribution. (Author's collection.)

F-12g 1279 is ready to leave DeWitt, New York, on July 17, 1943. Several rides aboard this engine with engineer Harry Doonan and fireman George Scharf hooked the author as a railroad enthusiast. It was a joy to watch the coordination of these men running this engine. This class of motive power was easy to fire and operate in any situation. Other crews felt the same. (Author's collection.)

F-12g 1285 is at an undisclosed location on the division. The numbering of the engine dates the picture post-1943, but an exact date and location are unknown. When leaving terminals, these engines were heaped with coal in their tenders. Fuel out on the railroad was just as important as water. (Author's collection.)

F-12g 1287 is seen in Utica, New York, on July 13, 1943, on another hot summer day. There were two enginehouses in Utica: one for the St. Lawrence and Adirondack Division motive power and the other for mainline power. (Author's collection.)

Unusual visitors from other parts of the railroad were hosted frequently. The engine pictured in Watertown, New York, on July 1, 1951, is D-1a 1295, recently renumbered and formerly the Boston & Albany (B&A) 400. Their appearance was brief as motive power for several passenger locals, which they were used to as commuter power in the Boston area. Time was closing in on them, with division dieselization close at hand. (Stoving/May collection.)

D-1a Boston & Albany 403 is pictured at Watertown, New York, on July 27, 1950. It was renumbered 1298 shortly after this photograph was taken. These engines had an extended frame supporting the tender as well as the locomotive. With a clear view coal bunker, they were bidirectional as well. A six-wheel truck supported the coal and water bunker. (Stoving/May collection.)

"Whitelined" for retirement is D-1a 1298, formerly the B&A 403, at Watertown, New York, on June 30, 1951. NYC did not go overboard on the new paint identification of the owner. Another unidentified engine worked 336/337, the Oswego-to-Syracuse local passenger train. Thirty-seven miles one way made it an ideal assignment. (Stoving/May collection.)

D-1a 1299, another former B&A acquisition, carries the number 404. This photograph is dated June 30, 1951, and the engine is now whitelined for off the roster and scrapping. (Stoving/May collection.)

B-10L 6609 is shown in Rome, New York, on June 13, 1943. The inclined cylinders and valve gear displayed on this engine were quite common on NYC motive power around the early 1900s. This engine was built in 1908. (Stoving/May collection.)

B-10v 6669 is pictured working the yard in Watertown, New York, on June 30, 1951. With diesel power taking over yard work and the total elimination of steam just months away, this old engine has had quite a career. (Stoving/May collection.)

B-10v 6707 is shown at the servicing area for steam near Arsenal Street, Watertown, New York, on August 26, 1950. Another alumnus of 1912. For many years during the more-modern steam era, some NYC power displayed six-window cabs on certain smaller engines. Presumably, the idea was to give better crew visibility. (Stoving/May collection.)

Heavier switching power needs were solved with the U-class engines such as U-2d 7376 at the enginehouse at Watertown, New York, on June 30, 1951. With all of the engine weight on the eight driving wheels, maximum traction was afforded. Clear view tenders were the norm for these engines, as well as the smaller B class. (Stoving/May collection.)

Seen here is U-2d 7333 at the Watertown, New York, enginehouse on August 26, 1950. It must be mentioned that engines of this class were frequently dispatched from here working local freights. Employee timetables restricted them to 30 mph. With no pilot or trailing trucks along with small diameter drivers, even 30 mph made for a wild ride. (Stoving/May collection.)

USRA U-3a 7825 is shown alongside the enginehouse in Watertown, New York, on July 1, 1951. The US Railway Administration (USRA) took over all of the US railroads during World War I. It also restricted all locomotive orders to their designs only. The designs were so good that even after the war and the end of USRA, it was rare to see any engine with modifications. (Stoving/May collection.)

U-3e 7909, another USRA engine, is shown at the Watertown enginehouse on August 27, 1950. Clean lines and mechanical details made these engines popular with the maintenance people. (Stoving/May collection.)

K-11e 4558 is shown at Utica, New York, on October 15, 1950. Built in the second decade of the 1900s for fast mainline freight hauling, they spent most of their later years working branch-line passenger runs as well as commuter work in the New York City area. Aptly suited for St. Lawrence Division as well as neighboring Adirondack lines, they performed their work very well. (Stoving/May collection.)

K-14g 4378 is pictured on the platform at Watertown, New York. The engine has an unusual background as having started service as a K-11f. It was later transferred to affiliate Boston & Albany, upgraded, and reclassified to K-14g status. The main difference pertained to larger 72-inch drivers from 69-inch originals. (Author's collection.)

K-3c 4827 is shown next to an engine facility in Massena, New York, on September 26, 1938. The engine-class history began in 1912, pulling mainline limiteds until the later Hudsons displaced them to secondary roles. Those 79-inch drivers were more than capable of high speeds. The engine was a rare Baldwin Locomotive Works product. (Stoving/May collection.)

K-3q 4680 rests at the enginehouse in Watertown, New York, on August 27, 1950. An American Locomotive Company product, it reveals those massive 79-inch drivers. Its running history would be interesting. (Stoving/May collection.)

H-5q 1372 is stored with its stack covered at enginehouse in Watertown, New York, on August 26, 1950. Coal showing in tender indicates it may be placed back in service if freight traffic picks up. This class of power numbered in the hundreds throughout the system with many differences in appliances, windows of cabs, and tenders. This engine was a home-built locomotive from the West Albany Shops in 1916. (Stoving/May collection.)

H-5La 1496 was stored at the Watertown, New York, engine facility on August 26, 1950, with a cap on its stack. Readily identified by its tender-carrying oil tank rather than a usual coal bunker, this engine was one of several that served trains entering the Adirondack Forest Preserve during the summer months to reduce fire hazard. For a while, they were converted back and forth, but that stopped when labor costs became too much. (Stoving/May collection.)

H-6a 1828 USRA Mikado with the 2-8-2 wheel arrangement similar to the H-5 class is pictured here in the snow of Watertown, New York, on November 26, 1949. NYC did one modification to this class. Coal boards were installed atop the tender to increase capacity by a couple of tons. This was an Alco product.

H-6a 1871 USRA poses at the enginehouse in Watertown, New York, on August 27, 1950. This was a Lima Locomotive Works product. (Stoving/May collection.)

H-6a 1880 USRA Mikado waits on the track at the Watertown, New York, enginehouse on August 27, 1950. Another Lima-built engine from 1918. Somehow, NYC tolerated bell mounting on smokebox front but preferred mid-boiler mounting to avoid icing in freezing weather. (Stoving/May collection.)

L-1b 2532 waits at Watertown, New York, on August 27, 1950. With a 4-8-2 wheel arrangement, they first appeared on the NYC in 1916, with this Alco product appearing in 1918. Speed on the mainline for freight trains was the intent. As the roster numbered into the hundreds, they found their way to the branch-line divisions. (Stoving/May collection.)

L-2d 2965 rests on the ready track in Watertown, New York, on August 27, 1950. These later-version Mohawks could take one by surprise, with a smokebox resembling a Hudson passenger locomotive front end. The 4-8-2 wheel arrangement spelled the difference as a high-speed freight locomotive. (Stoving/May collection.)

L-2d 2966 was another visitor to the Watertown, New York, enginehouse on July 1, 1951. St. Lawrence Division weight restrictions kept these big fellows only on the Syracuse/Massena and Rome/Richland lines. The 105-pound rail and improved bridges were the factors. While a few of the smaller classes had stokers, these engines had them as standard fare—a real treat for the firemen. (Stoving/May collection.)

L-2d 2969 is shown on enginehouse leads at Watertown, New York, on March 17, 1946. Their tenders should not be overlooked. Coal capacity was 28 tons, and water capacity consisted of 13,000 gallons. It is hard to believe these hardworking engines could consume a ton of coal every 15 miles. Stokers had to be a delight to these firemen after working the older non-equipped steam locomotives. (Stoving/May collection.)

The last revenue steam to run the St. Lawrence Division was the Huntington & Broad Top Railroad No. 38, a 2-8-0 wheel arrangement. Shown on home rails, this engine pulled the Syracuse chapter of the National Railway Historical Society (NRHS) excursion from Syracuse to Lacona in June 1954. The locomotive ended up at Rail City Museum nearby. (Author's collection.)

Shown just outside the single-stall enginehouse at Ottawa, Ontario, NYC F-12g 1272 awaits its crew in July 1949. Fires at wooden facilities such as this one were common. Fortunately for the railroad, these were self-insured. (Author's collection.)

Resting at the Watertown, New York, station platform, this July 1, 1951, photograph shows NYC U-2f 7560 resting between passenger car moves. Railing behind tender in the background further identifies the site as being adjacent to Black River. (Stoving/May collection.)

NYC F-12g 875 is shown at DeWitt, New York, in October 1946. It was later renumbered to 1285. The larger hand-me-down tender has replaced the original 7,500-gallon unit. The higher capacity could make a difference where intervals between servicing points were longer than usual. (Author's collection.)

The F-12g 876 is shown at the Canadian Pacific Railway enginehouse in Montreal, Quebec, Canada, in 1937. It was later renumbered to 1289. The trains were known to travel far distances, and it is possible it worked on trackage rights of the Rutland Railroad from Norwood to Malone, New York, and dispatched from there on the Adirondack Division to Montreal. Regardless, this engine was the last order of the F-12 class.

The NYC F-12g 872, renumbered to 1285, is shown at an unidentified location. Double-heading of this class of power was sometimes done on long heavy tonnage. (Stoving/May collection.)

The NYC F-12g 875, last renumbered to 1288, is shown adjacent to the enginehouse in Massena, New York, on September 26, 1938. These wood-framed structures were always vulnerable to fire for obvious reasons. Older style numbers and lettering are still evident. (Stoving/May collection.)

The F-12g 860, later renumbered 1273, is resting alongside the enginehouse in Ottawa, Ontario, Canada, on August 11, 1946. White flags indicate it worked an extra train from Helena, New York, this day. (Author's collection.)

The ATS-equipped F-12g 1277 is pictured at Utica, New York, on July 12, 1948. This was another engine providing preferred passenger and milk train service via Rome, Richland, and Watertown routing to the north country. (Author's collection.)

Pictured on September 4, 1946, the NYC F-12g 865, later renumbered 1278, has arrived in Ottawa, Ontario, Canada, with a passenger local carrying a postal car in its consist. One may wonder whether NYC had Canadian mail contracts besides the United States. The train was reputed to be a slow, sedate ride. (Author's collection.)

The NYC F-12e 1243 is shown at the DeWitt, New York, enginehouse on July 16, 1949. It makes one wonder how such a pristine machine can be retired and scrapped two years later. The crews loved their spunk and easy steaming qualities. (Author's collection.)

The NYC F-12e 1248 is shown at Utica, New York, on July 12, 1948, displaying freight pilot type on the front end. A grade crossing or derailment accident could have been the reason for a temporary replacement. (Author's collection.)

The NYC F-12e 1249 rests at the engine facility in Utica, New York, on October 15, 1950. This was another ATS-equipped engine that would be allowed 55 mph on the mainline to Rome with its train. None of the F-12s had valve pilot speed recorders, making one ponder about the habits of the enginemen. If only the engines could have talked! (Author's collection.)

Three

Diesel Power

The eventual conversion of steam to diesel power on the St. Lawrence Division was delayed somewhat with World War II. This might have been a mixed blessing in a certain respect. The various theories of economy and maintenance sounded good. Observation of other railroad's decision making and purchase of diesels probably saved the New York Central investment money in certain manufacturers and models that were not thoroughly proven for lengthy service.

Diesels for switching power had been purchased in the late 1930s and were disbursed around the railroad, including the St. Lawrence Division. The concept of a locomotive being shut down after use was one of the most important selling concepts. With steam, one did not have that concept, as the locomotive had to be attended to 24 hours a day regardless of it working or sitting at a terminal awaiting another assignment. Naturally, fuel economy was another factor.

With the postwar period uptick in railroad business, as well as very reliable diesel power from five principal manufacturers being available, the die was cast. It was theorized that the diesel potential could reduce the steam roster of the railroad by four-fifths. How 2,000 diesel purchases could replace 10,000 steam seemed and sounded impossible. And how could it be done and not duplicate existing servicing facilities?

The concept was moving steam from eastern divisions starting on the Boston & Albany Division. As more diesels arrived, steam would be retired if close to major class repairs and scrapped. Serviceable steam would be pushed westward to other divisions. The St. Lawrence Division received some expatriate engines, as will be described in a later chapter.

It required a little more time, but late 1951 had the St. Lawrence Division totally dieselized. There was some sadness from the senior enginemen but also relief regarding the responsibilities of safe operation.

The diesels brought some interesting observations and stories as they took over. Four different manufacturers had locomotives operating on the division at various times. A fifth player was the Lima Locomotive Works but was never recorded as being in operation per author records.

Baldwin and Fairbanks Morse were minor players in the diesel market. Alco and the EMD (Electro-Motive Diesel) portion of General Motors were the favored suppliers. They produced some locomotive models that received many duplicate orders.

NYC 9303, a Baldwin V01000 switcher in later years of service, is pictured at an undisclosed location. Frequent assignment to ST5/6 working out of DeWitt, it put its muscle into some surprising tonnage. A non-turbocharged eight-cylinder engine with a bore and stroke of 12-3/4 by 15-1/2 coupled with Westinghouse electrical gear performed the magic. Rated at 1,000 horsepower, they were impressive in operation. (Author's collection.)

NYC 8607, later renumbered 9307, works at the Watertown, New York, depot early in its career. Passenger car switching was relatively light duty. Visors on front and rear headlights gave them a brutish look. Four exhaust stacks are barely visible over the top of the hood. Never mentioned in other Baldwin commentary was their sound similar to an old Bendix washing machine. They were also rough riders out on the road, causing one to wonder whether they had any springs in the trucks. (Author's collection.)

NYC 9328, a Baldwin S-12 switcher, works at an undisclosed location, packing a six-cylinder turbocharged engine of the same bore and stroke as the V01000s. The photograph must have been made late in its career as the white stripe was done on all switchers for safety on crossings at night. Early in its career, a monthly inspection in the cab revealed work taken place at Benson Mines, New York, on the Newton Falls branch—the perfect assignment for this locomotive. (Author's collection.)

NYC 9324, another S-12 Baldwin switcher, is pictured at an undisclosed location. It was frequently seen working the division on ST5/6. The front of the engine has a rolled-up canvas radiator cover to protect the engine in freezing weather. Six of these S-12s (9323-9328) worked the division. (Author's collection.)

The freshly washed NYC Alco S-2 8584 frequently worked in Oswego, New York. It was amazing how a turbocharger increased horsepower by one-third. Passed along to Penn-Central and Conrail, they reflected their design and reliability to survive 50 years of service.

NYC Alco RS-3 8241 and RDC M-463 await departures from Massena, New York, on an unknown winter date, perhaps sometime during the late 1950s, based on the equipment paint. Safety stripes on the RDC (rail diesel car) did not embellish its appearance but did cut down the number of grade-crossing accidents. The Massena depot is in the background. (Author's collection.)

NYC Alco FA-2 1060 was another frequent visitor to the division and was always coupled to as many as five units to get the tonnage delivered. Other make units could be in the consist, which made for interesting photography. (Author's collection.)

NYC Alco RS-3 8253 is shown at DeWitt, New York, near the enginehouse. It was built with the same prime mover as the FA-2 but with a different car body, a train heating boiler in a short hood, and switcher capability. Popular with engine crews, it could tackle any assignment. (Author's collection.)

NYC Alco RS-3 8336 was another division visitor shown at an unknown location in the late 1950s, before the austere black paint scheme that would follow. With the elimination of passenger service system-wide, the engine shows having its train heating boiler removed by no stack on the short hood.

NYC Alco FA-1/FB-1 freight diesels demonstrating as delivered with three-fourths striping on "A" units and no stripe on "B" (booster engine). The location was Adams Center, New York, where a double track from Watertown ended at the switch stand in the foreground. A photogenic crew takes advantage of the moment.

This is a rare photograph of the engine facility at Massey Yard, Watertown, New York, in the early 1960s, depicting a set of Alco freight units in what was called a cigar paint scheme. It may have been economical but hardly becoming to the company's former image. A late-model Ford to the left helps date the photograph. (Author's collection.)

A later paint scheme on one of a group of six EMD FTAs coupled with FTB at an undisclosed location. They covered the railroad as demonstrators, proving their worth in critical areas. With only six pairs in the order, they were frequent visitors to the division. Their distinctive paint scheme made them a hit with the general public. (Author's collection.)

X8005 NYC Rail Detector Car was a frequent visitor to the division, analyzing rail for internal defects not seen by the human eye. The internal cracks and fissures could cause a derailment. With older light rail on so many branches, its frequent use on a regular basis saved the railroad great expense. (Author's collection.)

A surprise visitor on ST5/6 in 1956 was this Fairbanks Morse H-20-44 transfer switcher. Boasting 2,000 horsepower, the 19 units purchased were very successful at every assignment given them. In 1949, a half dozen of them came to the division and were assigned to different locations where high horsepower tractive effort could make a difference. Unfortunately, they were transferred elsewhere for better utilization. (Author's collection.)

This is a rare photograph of the fueling plant servicing diesels at DeWitt, New York. Looking east, there is a collection of yard power in the foreground that was recorded operating on the division at various dates. Engine crews for the St. Lawrence Division boarded their engines here. (NYCSHS.)

Deadheading in train consist of OFD 2, Alco RS-3 8299 decided to part company with a half dozen cars in a derailment north of Fulton, New York, in 1962. The location had recently been purchased from the New York Ontario & Western Railroad, which went bankrupt in 1957. A light wrecking crane had its work cut out, lifting a locomotive nearly its own weight. (Author's collection.)

Four

Passenger Trains

During the 1940s, the St. Lawrence Division maintained passenger service on most of its branch lines. Improved highways and greater use of automobiles were starting to make an impact on revenues. Various experiments had started in the 1930s to reduce overhead on the branches with gas-electric railcars, skirting the full crew laws found on conventional trains. Lucrative postal contracts for carrying mail in railway postal cars were still found on many of the trains. The region was also rich in milk production going to the New York City markets. The use of express refrigerator cars specifically equipped for high-speed service was other headend equipment.

Pullman destinations on the division were probably record holders for any non-mainline New York Central division. The upstate cities served were Watertown, Ogdensburg, Massena, and Oswego. Seasonal Pullman service was also sent to the resort area of Clayton, the gateway to the Thousand Islands. This service was a through train from New York City.

The railroad provided the most efficient and fastest service to the north country. Despite the length of the routes, there was not any dining car service. Instead, a restaurant in the depot at Richland served several trains. Meal stops were usually 15 minutes long. Coach service was on all of the passenger routes to accommodate the general public. Many were used on the Massena train weekends and holidays to serve the students at Canton and Potsdam Universities. It was affectionately called the "Canton Creeper" because of all its intermediate stops.

The Syracuse/Massena car was an oddity for the Pullman Company, as it was exclusively for the Alcoa Aluminum plant in Massena. Originally going to New York City, the NYC railroad rerouted the car on a westbound train to Ashtabula, Ohio, then transferring it to a subsidiary train of the Pittsburgh & Lake Erie for the remainder of the trip to Pittsburgh. It was probably the oddest route and referred to as the "nowhere to nowhere."

As late as the early 1950s, there were a couple of mixed trains working on the St. Lawrence Division. They covered the Clayton and Cape Vincent branches. Other than newspaper clippings, no photos were found evidencing their operation. It was noted in the clippings the combination baggage/coach and postal mail cars had chimneys meaning they were heated with potbelly coal stoves for minimum comfort in the winter weather. These trains were the end of railroad history, going back to the 1800s, stopping everywhere to drop off or pick up freight cars along the way. For passengers, patience was important as schedules were rarely adhered to.

It will be noted that at least one gas-electric car worked the Ogdensburg/DeKalb Junction line in the 1950s to afford passenger connections with Syracuse-bound trains.

The Ogdensburg/Utica train, in later years, took a zig-zag route by way of Philadelphia/Watertown/Carthage to attract more coach and Pullman traffic in Watertown. While Ogdensburg had much industry and citizen patronage, there was another group to be mentioned. Ogdensburg was the seat of the Roman Catholic Diocese of Northern New York. With the constant need for roundtrip travel of clergy and personnel to New York City, they were important patrons as well.

Still active until the mid-1940s was a summer-only through Pullman and coach train from New York City to Clayton, a resort town on the St. Lawrence River and gateway to the Thousand Islands. It was the only division train to offer food service en route. A postcard illustrates the multiple tracks at the Clayton depot for arriving trains and storage for layover cars.

It is important to mention the well-heeled patrons that rode this route. With only a few steps at Clayton to private or public watercraft, they were transported short distances to their island retreats of great luxury that most likely matched the owners' offseason residences.

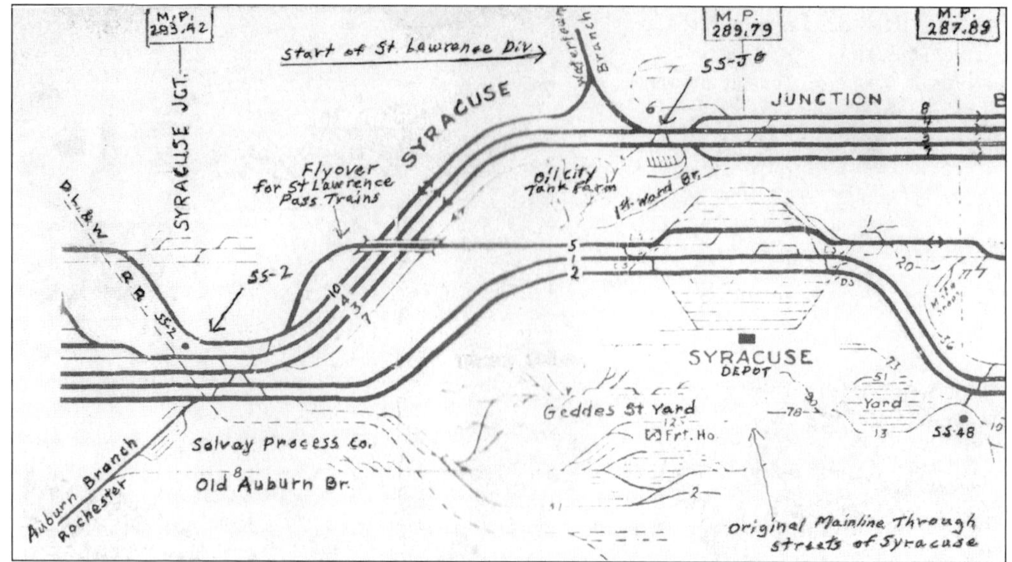

This is a condensed map of the Syracuse, New York, trackage demonstrating how the St. Lawrence Division passenger trains could enter or leave the depot without delay from all the mainline trains. Trains left and entered the station in reverse on track No. 5.

Pictured here is the No. 189 Utica/Ogdensburg passenger train at Hammond, New York. The train consist was operated in reverse northbound, as turning facilities at Ogdensburg had been removed. Smoke from Alco RS-3 was typical when accelerating from stations. (Author's collection.)

The NYC RS-3 8253 is shown ready to leave Massena on May 19, 1961, heading to Syracuse. A sleeper car to Pittsburgh is attached at the rear of the train. (Author's collection.)

Declining passenger revenue prompted the NYC to try a different approach to passenger service on branch lines. The Budd Company in Philadelphia, Pennsylvania, developed a stainless-steel self-propelled RDC to help meet the problem. Powered by two General Motors truck diesel engines developing 275 horsepower each and transferring power to the wheels through torque converters, they offered modern convenience as well as air-conditioning. A few of them had baggage compartments for checked baggage. They were moderately popular until the ax finally fell on all passenger service in the 1960s. Pictured are passengers discharging from the Budd RDC-1 at the Watertown depot in the mid-1950s. (Courtesy of Jefferson County Historical Society.)

The NYC Budd RDC M-458 is pictured at the Roots Block station beyond Watertown. The RDC is northbound, receiving train orders, and is officially on the timetable as train 609. (NYCSHS.)

The division hauled US Army troop trains from Syracuse to Camp Drum (now Fort Drum) just north of Watertown. The siding to the military installation was at Roots, New York, hardly more than a railroad location. Movements of trains were usually highly classified. In earlier days, the consists were heavyweight Pullman cars with an Army commissary car inserted mid-train for meals. During the steam era, mainline power was required to pull the heavy trains. Diesels in multiple units were used later. Pictured here are the NYC GP-7s 5790 and 5789 northbound entering the military siding. (NYCSHS.)

Pictured here are both the left and the right of the NYC 832, which was later renumbered as 1245. The train is switching passenger cars at Oswego in September 1941. (Author's collection.)

The NYC motor car M-404 at Ogdensburg on August 22, 1946. The unit handled local passenger runs from Ogdensburg to DeKalb junction for several years. This was another economy train for the division. (Author's collection.)

The NYC F12g-class 1286 and 1280 are shown here double-heading as they await the Rochester chapter of the NRHS patrons on track 11 of the depot on September 17, 1950. The railfan excursion would proceed to SS-29 before heading north to Charlotte, then west to the Suspension Bridge. Since the excursion was operated on the former Rome, Watertown & Ogdensburg Railroad (RW&O) track from Charlotte, the St. Lawrence Division crews would operate the train. (Author's collection.)

This is another view of the Rochester railfan excursion trip in September 1950. The passengers have detrained for run by somewhere on the branch to the Suspension Bridge. The passengers always liked action and smoke for a photo opportunity. (Author's collection.)

The NYC 832, later renumbered as 1245, is shown here in August 1940. The train was on a Niagara Falls fan trip from Rochester. (Author's collection.)

New York Central Railroad

NON-TRANSFERABLE, REDUCED FARE, SPECIAL ROUND TRIP TICKET

GOOD ONLY FOR ONE CONTINUOUS PASSAGE

SYRACUSE to HEUVELTON, N. Y.

In consideration of the reduced fare at which this ticket is sold, it will be good for a CONTINUOUS PASSAGE when stamped by Agent on back hereof and journey must be commenced so as to reach original starting point before midnight of date punched out in margin hereof.

Baggage will be transported subject to tariff regulations.

Any erasure or alteration on this ticket or if more than one date is punched out renders it void.

Not good on certain Limited Trains.

J. W. Switzer
Gen'l Passenger Agent

Form S. R. T. 1

1935 1936 1937 1938 1939 1940 1941 1942 1943 1944 1945

A 33930

JAN FEB MAR APR MAY JUN JUL AUG SEP OCT NOV DEC 31 30 29 28 27 26 25 24 23 22

DAY 1 2 3 4 5 6 7 8 9 10 11 12 13 14 15 16 17 18 19 20 21

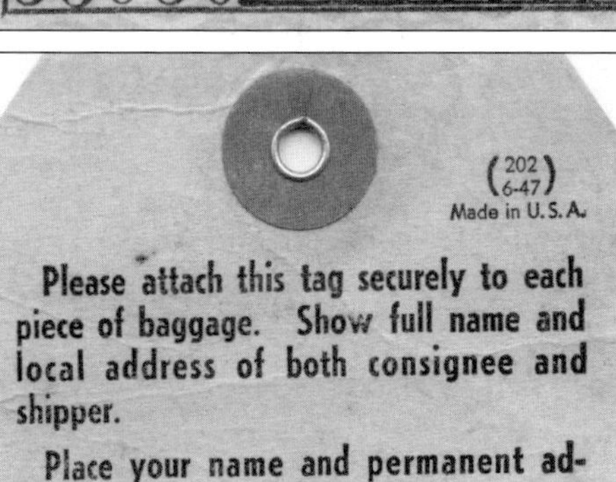

(202 6-47)
Made in U.S.A.

Please attach this tag securely to each piece of baggage. Show full name and local address of both consignee and shipper.

Place your name and permanent address inside each piece of baggage.

Money, Jewelry, Silverware, Precious Stones, should not be inclosed in baggage. They should be shipped separately and a special department is provided for forwarding such articles.

Passenger tickets and luggage tags were issued when riding aboard the passenger trains, as shown here. The ticket above is good for one continuous passage from Syracuse to Heuvelton, New York. A luggage tag was included on each piece of luggage.

The F-12g 867, later renamed 1280, is pictured in Philadelphia at an unknown date. It is presumably a Clayton Local making a passenger connection.

New York, April 25, 1951

Mr. C. F. Grimes:

Your letter April 23rd, File D-96,

Effective Sunday, April 29th, (new time table), arrange to hold train 140 at Syracuse until 11:00 AM in the event St.Lawrence Division train 10 is late.

C. E. Black.

Copy GHB CEB DTH GCN FJP JCH EBF JWM FCF ERD CLP WBG GX NIGHT FORCE.

Frequent bulletins between division superintendents were necessary to insure passenger and Pullman connections at Syracuse, New York, such as this one. In this bulletin, the St. Lawrence Division superintendent was addressing the Syracuse Division superintendent. Revenue from possible milk and mail traffic was another priority. Lack of coordination between these two officials could be costly.

N. Y. C. S.
T 100

FORM 19 (Made in U. S. A.) FORM 19

NEW YORK CENTRAL SYSTEM

TRAIN ORDER NO. 311

Aug 15 1957

To C. and E. No 59 At Philadelphia

X .... Opr.; .... M.

Regular trains due
Philadelphia before 720
seven two naught am
August 15th have
departed
J D

Conductor and Engineman must each have a copy of this order.

Made Complete Time 723a M. Allinsen Opr.

Pictured here is a train order for northbound passenger No. 59 Utica/Ogdensburg.

Five

FREIGHT SERVICE

There were very few towns and cities served by the St. Lawrence Division that were not revenue producers for the railroad. Manufactured as well as raw goods gave great diversity to the region. With the bankruptcy of the New York, Ontario & Western Railway (NYO&W) in 1957, the NYC picked up a couple of major industries in Fulton.

Several pages could be written about the train and the crews moving trains uphill and loaded ones coming south. Two of these trains were officially called PB-1 and BP-2; the letters stood for Benson Mines and Pittsburgh. Ore, the most unusual mined product, of little fanfare to the general public, was probably the highest density material to be transported. The open-top hopper cars were to the limit of weight allowed when only filled to slightly more than one-third cubic feet of capacity. When moving on a train, the cars jiggled like Jell-O. Speeds of trains were limited.

US Geological Survey (USGS) maps of the area around Benson Mines indicate considerable trackage inside the mining area where trains could turn around for the southbound trip. Before loading, the ore was scintered in a heating process and loaded hot in the cars.

Southbound ore movements were the real test for the train crews. Before leaving Benson Mines, there would be a brake test, and sufficient retaining valves were turned up on the cars. The diesels had the advantage over steam by having dynamic braking to help control the speed on the downhill run to Carthage. At the discretion of the engineer, the train would stop at Harrisville for another inspection.

As the branch into Watertown from Carthage would involve street running, the train went northward to Philadelphia, where it wyed to the southbound Massena/Syracuse line to Watertown. Stopping at Massey Yard, the train would undergo another inspection. As the cars were mostly equipped with solid bearings, overheating could be a constant threat with the possibility of a derailment if not caught in time. Despite all these precautions, ore trains were restricted to 30–35 mph on the entire railroad.

Leaving Watertown, the train continued south to Syracuse. At SS-JG, the end of the division, instead of going east to DeWitt Yard, it went west to the Belle Isle Yard, where there would be a crew change and inspection.

There was another symbol freight train: MU-2 and UM-1. Originally operated on the Adirondack Division between Utica and Montreal, its route was changed when the division was segmented from Lake Clear Junction to Malone in the 1950s. The later route was from Malone to Norwood on trackage rights of the Rutland Railroad. The train carried perishables in refrigerated cars. Crews referred to it as "the Banana Train." Having priority status, it wasted no time getting over the division.

ST-7/8 (DeWitt to Oswego) via Pulaski was another significant train handling mostly coal for the lakeside power plant at Oswego. Consists of around 180 cars were frequent in number, with all eastern roads represented. What was fascinating were the build dates on many of the cars, indicating 04, 06, and 07. With the abandonment of the Pulaski to Paul (Oswego) branch, the train was rerouted on the Phoenix line from Woodard. The NYO&W portion of the line acquired in 1957 was still laid with its 65-pound rail and made the operation very interesting.

ST 5/6 (DeWitt to Fulton) did local work from Liverpool to Fulton and picked up empties and loads on its way back to DeWitt. A favorite of train crews because of its overtime. The end-of-week train carried deadhead switchers to Fulton. With the demise of the NYO&W, the NYC picked up two important freight accounts served by five different day and evening switching jobs in Fulton.

This photograph was taken around 1945 at an unknown location on the division and depicts a four-unit EMD combination of FT diesels in the original paint scheme from the factory. Fortunately, they were repainted soon after into a more-pleasing lighting stripe that made them quite distinctive in appearance. (Courtesy of the Jefferson County Historical Society.)

NYC U-2d 0-3-0 7376 is shown doing yard work at Norwood, New York, as steam power was coming to a close. Norwood was an interchange point with the Rutland Railroad and also the Norwood & St. Lawrence, a shortline railroad. It served a large pulp mill in Waddington, New York, 18 miles away on the St. Lawrence River. (Author's collection.)

A very pristine NYC 19000 series caboose is shown at Massena, New York, after shopping around 1960. Many of these cabooses served almost 60 years of service. Often wrecked and rebuilt several times, they were finally retired. Crews referred to them as "the little home away from home." Potbelly stoves provided not only heat, but also a flat surface for cooking. Rear marker protection had changed to more-economical discs, replacing kerosene lamps.

Southbound NYC BP-2 with four Alco FA diesel units are shown leaving Adams Center, New York, after climbing the grade from Watertown. A mile marker indicates 63 miles to Syracuse. A White (make) truck completes the scene.

Shown at the Route 11 crossing in Pulaski, New York, in a winter scene of the late 1950s, a northbound freight train was utilizing the brief double track to Richland, New York. (Author's collection.)

NYC Alco FA-1 1040 is leading three other units in a consist, under the Arsenal Street bridge in Watertown, New York, in the early 1950s with the ore train BP-2. The track to the extreme left was the beginning of the Limerick branch going to Cape Vincent, New York. (NYCSHS.)

A block operator in Roots, New York, hands up train orders to the fireman on Alco RS-3 8306, powering the Carthage Turn. Almost six miles north of Watertown, it was also the junction of the spur going into the military reservation known as Camp Drum, now Fort Drum. (NYCSHS.)

A station operator at Adams Center, New York, is about to demonstrate the art of handing up train orders to the engineer. The exercise was sometimes referred to as "hooping orders." Two sets were always used; one was handed to the engine crew, and the other to the conductor on the caboose. Alco RS-3s are heading the long train. (NYCSHS.)

NYC GP-7s 5763 and 5762 are shown leaving Adams Center, New York, with a southbound freight train for DeWitt Yard at Syracuse. Consecutive numbers on engines are fair clues to recent factory deliveries, dating this photograph to 1953. (NYCSHS.)

A northbound freight is receiving train orders at Adams Center, New York. The engineer is a longtime friend of the author, Don Robarge, working the extra board. Don Robarge was hired in 1941 and later promoted. (NYCSHS.)

The conductor on the same northbound train receives his copy of train orders at Adams Center, New York. What makes a train official is the display of marker lights on the rear-most rolling stock. (NYCSHS.)

Consaul-Hall Coal Co., located in Clayton, New York, provided fuel to the steamships on the St. Lawrence River. A valued freight customer of the NYC, it ceased operations when diesel-powered ships took over.

Northbound freight DFO-1 leaves Woodard, New York, on Phoenix branch with three Alco engines as road power. Deadheading behind are two Alco switchers that are the Monday swap for Fulton and Oswego yard work.

The St. Lawrence Division operated some unique freight cars as this open-top boxcar represents. They were used for pulpwood, with the doors closed before loading. A number of paper mills on division received these 36-foot cars and, later, 40-foot USRA steel cars. Inside, a ladder is visible through the open door, permitting workers to enter.

Six

St. Lawrence Division Depots

The depots pictured on the following pages reflect the cross-section of the entire division. The absorption of many shortline railroads by the former Rome, Watertown & Ogdensburg and, later, New York Central contributed to the flavor of architecture in the remaining structures. Proudly, many survivors are in private hands with little modification.

Sizable communities served had brick and stone depots to compliment the prospective patronage and traffic. The remaining wooden structures are sizable in number, with readily identifiable NYC architecture. A favorite, and probably the smallest depot on the division, is at Brownville on the former Cape Vincent branch.

Fire was always a possibility in the early years of the division. Perhaps it explains the oddness of the depot in Lacona, south of Watertown.

The Fulton (Broadway) and Phoenix depots, now razed, were two-story structures. Upstairs was the agent's quarters when other accommodations were not available. It is possible that certain depots were moved to other locations by private owners.

A postcard of Clayton, New York, shows the depot and tracks for passenger trains during the heyday of summer traffic in the early 20th century for Thousand Island resort guests. A hand-operated turntable was located to the right of the picture for turning engine power.

N.Y.C. BRIDGE OVER BARGE CANAL AND OSWEGO RIVER, OSWEGO, N. Y.

9626

Pictured is an eastbound passenger train leaving Oswego station and crossing the namesake river 200 feet away. The train was most likely the No. 48, a local to Utica via Pulaski via Richland and Rome. The express milk car behind the locomotive indicates an area producer and shipper.

The Chaumont, New York, depot was 13.06 miles from Watertown on the Cape Vincent branch. This early postcard shows a station with a shed for patrons to stand under during the busy summer months.

The Cornwall, Ontario, Canada, depot is 62.29 miles from Tupper Lake junction. The customs building is where the depot sign hangs. It was once a part of the New York & Ottawa Division before 1936 abandonment south of Helena, New York. The Canadian portion remained active.

The depot at Carthage, New York, is seen here in 2006. The station is 74.34 miles north of Utica and also served east to west Falls trains going from Watertown to Newton.

This is a 2006 street view of the Carthage, New York, station. It was open 24 hours a day as a block station as well.

The Lyons Fall, New York, station, pictured here in 2006, was 44.80 miles from Utica. This is typical NYC-style architecture, and the major customer here was Gould Paper Co.

The Phoenix, New York, depot was 8.38 miles from Woodard. This 1910 photograph shows the second story that was living quarters for the agent.

This is a 1920s postcard illustrating the Oswego, New York, station. The depot is located 25.04 miles west of Pulaski. The city could be reached by NYC from three directions.

Above is a postcard of the Watertown, New York, depot and the division headquarters. This is an unusual view of the station, as during this time, the Hotel Woodruff would otherwise have obstructed the view. The station is 71.10 miles north of Syracuse. Located in the center of town, the train station closing in the 1960s was also the beginning of the demise of the hotel. Below is the rearview of the Watertown station showing the platforms.

New York Central Station, New Haven, N. Y.

The New Haven, New York, depot was located 13.04 miles from Pulaski. The depot was close to the shore of Lake Ontario and was a stop for a former NYC president who had a summer home there. He also kept a private car at the station for such visits.

The Pulaski, New York, station was a combination depot and freight house. This allowed for service for both passengers and freight. The depot was at the junction with a line going west to Oswego. (Author's collection.)

The Adams, New York, depot was 57.38 miles from Syracuse. This is another view of a classic structure in the NYC architecture style.

Seen here is a 1910 postcard of Pierrepont Manor, New York, depot. This depot was 51.68 miles from Syracuse. The area was named after William Constable Pierrepont, who was well known for many business deals, including the development of the first railroad, the Watertown & Rome, into northern New York.

This 1920s postcard illustrates the Dekalb Junction, New York, depot, a combination depot and freight house. Dekalb Junction was 18.91 miles from the Ogdensburg branch and 121.14 miles from Syracuse.

The Felt Mills, New York, depot, photographed c. 1920, was located 8.66 miles east of Watertown on the Black River. The town was named after John Felts, who started the mill industry. (Author's collection.)

This is a 2006 photograph of the Lacona, New York, depot, 45.20 miles from Syracuse. Built in 1891, it was listed in the National Register of Historic Places in 2002. The structure has been renovated but still retains its railroad charm. (Author's collection.)

This 2006 photograph of the Adams Center, New York, depot, is looking north toward Watertown. It was the beginning of a double-track descending into Black River Valley. The depot is 61.13 miles north of Syracuse and also a cutoff point for freight pushers on southbound freight trains. (Author's collection.)

This is a 2006 photograph of the Evans Mills, New York, depot, 81.10 miles from Syracuse. The repurposed depot and freight house is still standing, displaying its heritage.

The West Yard office in Oswego, New York, was the last surviving structure in the yard complex. The yard activities ended in 1985. Below is a rear view of the West Yard office.

Seen here is a 2006 view of the Cape Vincent, New York, depot on the St. Lawrence River, now a marina. This was the exit for train passengers traveling to Canada by boat. It was located at the end of the branch from Watertown, 24.68 miles east.

The Holland Patent, New York, depot was 12.12 miles north of Utica on the Ogdensburg line. It is privately owned and retains its originality, including paint, as seen in this 2006 photograph.

The Brownville, New York, depot is 4.82 miles from Watertown on the Cape Vincent branch. It is probably the smallest depot on the division.

The Lowville, New York, depot is 58.73 miles from Utica. Considerable modifications have been made by the recent owner. The concrete platform indicates there was heavy passenger and express traffic in years past.

Shown above and below is the Castorland, New York, depot, which is 65.91 miles from Utica. The depot appears to be abandoned in this photograph from 2006, and it is possible it no longer is in existence.

Shown here is the Harrisville, New York, depot located 20.62 miles from Carthage. This was the first station on the Newton Falls branch inside the Adirondack Forest Preserve. As of 2006, the Town of Diana Historical Museum was occupying the space. (Author's collection.)

The Sacketts Harbor depot was located 11.04 miles from Watertown. Adjacent to the pier, passenger trains could transfer patrons to boats going to Canada. More recently, it became a restaurant. (Author's collection.)

The Mexico, New York, depot and freight house was located 8.53 miles from Pulaski on the Oswego branch. The railroad crossed the highway on the left side of the utility pole. Below is the rear view of the depot in 2006. The NYC tried to construct stations on the basis of the number of potential patrons, both public and corporate.

The McConnellsville, New York, freight house is 17.27 miles from Utica. This is the typical freight house design, with an extended roofline. (Author's collection.)

The Camden, New York, depot and freight house is located 22.01 miles from Utica. With the cessation of milk traffic due to faster options and refrigeration, this branch line became segmented from Camden to Richland and was later totally abandoned. (Author's collection.)

The Potsdam, New York, freight house was 139.92 miles to Syracuse. The size of the structure indicates freight patronage. According to the Potsdam Public Museum website, in the 1980s, the freight station was used by Montgomery Ward for storage.

The Heuvelton, New York, depot was located 7.23 miles from Ogdensburg. This area was known for its heavy milk production and was most likely the main function of transportation for this station.

The freight house in Gouverneur, New York, was 106.04 miles from Syracuse. This 2006 photograph indicates new siding for an NYC classic structure.

The Massena, New York, depot is located 158.63 miles from Syracuse. The depot is close to the Canadian border and an interchange point with the Canadian National Railroad.

The Ogdensburg, New York, freight house is 134.43 miles from Utica. The original is a stone structure, and the additional wood-frame structure later added is visible.

The Booneville, New York, depot is 34.86 miles from Utica. This area is known as the coldest winter location in the state of New York. The concrete platform was used for passenger patronage.

The Booneville, New York, freight house was located a distance from the depot and on the opposite side of the track.

The Norwood, New York, depot is located 145.99 miles from Syracuse. This 1948 view of the No. 8 Massena/Syracuse passenger train with a K-11 engine is about to make a platform stop. The train had just crossed Rutland Railroad's main track to Ogdensburg.

This turn-of-the-century view of the depot at Watertown, New York, with the Railway Expres building at the left. It was an impressive location for the many years the division headquarters was located there. (Courtesy of Jefferson County Historical Society.)

This is a photograph of the Woodard, New York, depot looking north on the Watertown main track. The junction of the Oswego branch is to the left of the depot but not pictured. Years earlier, there was a wye track beyond the bridge, which was mostly used by switching crews for positioning of boxcars to be unloaded on a particular side. (Author's collection.)

This is a pre-1948 photograph of the depot and freight house with an engine facility at Ottawa, Ontario. The double doors to the right indicate that once it was a two-stall affair. The construction of the St. Lawrence Seaway in 1956 severed the line from Helena, New York, ending the freight service to Ottawa by the NYC. (Author's collection.)

This is another pre-1948 photograph of the Ottawa, Ontario, depot and freight house. The F-12g 865, later 1278, sits outside. The baggage car and unmarked boxcar were probably part of the consist of the mixed train operating to Helena, New York, at this time. The tracks in the foreground are Canadian Pacific, giving credence to the remark by railroaders of the NYC about entering Ottawa through the back door.

Seven

PERSONALITIES

Even in 1940, the hiring of enginemen on the railroad was not much different from decades earlier. Physique and intelligence were key ingredients of any candidate. On the NYC, a prospective fireman, before hiring, had to make three apprentice trips with a road freight crew. There were unpaid trips as well. It required being under the direction of the fireman and doing all of the work in maintaining steam from shoveling coal into a hungry firebox. Proper footing atop a jarring deck plate was necessary. The engineer would sign off after each successful trip.

The next phase required knowing the mechanical parts of the steam locomotive, studying division maps to remember passing siding lengths, and understanding the Book of Rules conduct. There would be a written test covering all of the material.

The successful candidate, having passed everything, would await their first call to work, which would be the beginning of a seniority date. A first trip was always one of apprehension, wondering about the engineer's sympathy for a new hire. There were those who could make life difficult for a new fireman by working the engine extra hard and requiring continuous attention to the level of fire, plus keeping water in the boiler at a working level.

Most of the engineers were easy to work for and could offer great advice if there was a problem. There were a few scoundrels whose reputations preceded them, and they will be mentioned later. It takes all kinds of personalities to run a railroad and, some of the hilarious characters are featured in this chapter.

One of the high-seniority engineers who could have been a PR man for the railroad was **Harry Doonan (hired November 4, 1906)**. Whenever he arrived at a branch-line town to take on water and oil the valve gear, curious youngsters would appear to watch his magic. After finishing, he would walk over and oil their bicycle chains, talk, and sometimes hand out candy. He was a tall figure and kind of a folk hero to them.

George Alexander (hired March 30, 1910) was another skilled engineman who accepted the diesels with some reluctance. He was of the old railroad type of thinking regarding steam versus diesel. During the time I knew him, George described the inner workings of some of the lesser-make diesels like a salesman and with humor.

Monikers were common on the railroad, and the St. Lawrence Division had its share of them. Most of them came as rewards for outstanding (if not unusual) personality. Several are mentioned in this chapter.

John "Smiling Jack" Bragger (hired August 20, 1916) was one of the more interesting engineers. Not that he intended it, as his words were few, but when utterances came, they were always original. Legend had it that Jack only smiled once in his life—the day a certain inlay passed. Engine failure out on the road would never be blamed on Bragger, as he was a mechanical genius on steam as well as diesel.

On a Saturday in the late 1950s, Bragger was assigned a Baldwin VO switcher for a freight turn. Taking these veteran engines out on the road was a gamble. This night would become memorable. The engine prime mover would periodically stop, and restarting it would be challenging. Finally, it quit for good at a junction depot where there was a direct line to a nearby enginehouse. All the train crew followed Bragger into the depot. The block operator hooked up the dispatcher line to the enginehouse using a telephone that had a scissors-type mouthpiece swinging out from the wall and headphones that allowed one to hear the other party. To speak, the user pressed down on a foot pedal. Fortunately, there was a speaker on the wall, so they could hear the other end of the conversation. The conversation began with Bragger explaining the problem, how long it would take to fix it, the parts necessary to complete the job, and the number of mechanics to attend to the problem. From the calm nature of the master mechanic on the other end of the phone, one could probably tell he had his feet up on the desk. His replies were "Yes, Jack," "Okay, Jack," "All right, Jack," and finally, "Is there anything else, Jack?" Bragger hunched down into the mouthpiece and bellowed, "Yeah, bring me a new left hand! I wore the other one out punchin' the GD starter button!" The crew got up and walked out the back door. Bragger had struck again!

Bragger briefly worked an evening switching job in Oswego. One of his comical firemen commented it was not as fun working the day job, as he missed the fireworks display shoving loaded coal hoppers up the ramp to the Delaware, Lackawanna & Western (DL&W) Railroad coal dock. The stunning display resulted from 90 mph wheel slips of a Fairbanks Morse H-16-44 road switcher.

John "Banjo Eyes" Kellogg (hired February 24, 1920) was another engineer legend. His moniker was earned by the extremely large eyeglass lenses he wore at one time. Kellogg was full of tall stories causing you to study each one before digesting it.

Kellogg was the only engineer interviewed that actually ran a Niagara steam locomotive on the division. This mainline passenger locomotive was restricted on most of the division because of its weight. The occasion was because of a mainline derailment between Rome and Syracuse. A detour was selected on the St. Lawrence Division of Rome/Richland/Syracuse. Boarding the Niagara pulling the Empire State Express at Utica, he assumed the throttle at Rome for his portion of the trip. He admitted running 70 mph on a 55 mph track. His last comment was, "Had the track gang realigning rail for two weeks after that trip."

John Kellogg's other notable adventure was during a union strike at the General Electric plant at Liverpool. Their electrical workers union members were tough negotiators, and scenes of violence were frequent. During strikes, guard towers were erected, and the plant looked more like a fortress. During one of these episodes, Kellogg and his train crew had a boxcar to leave inside the plant. As he and his crew were union people, they would not violate another's picket line. Leaving the train crew with their train, he proceeded up the siding with the engine and car. Within a couple hundred feet of the gate, he stopped and motioned for a guard to come over to the engine. Waving him up into the cab, he quizzed him whether he had ever run a locomotive. Getting a negative reply, he told him he was going to give him a crash exam. Kellogg told him he was getting off, so the guard had to take the engine and car through the gate, uncouple the car, and bring the engine back to them. It was a strange arrangement, not exactly by the book, but the delivery was made.

On another job, Kellogg worked with a fireman who was always worried whether his car would start after finishing work at DeWitt. Kellogg told him not to worry, as he would put the car in the back seat of his Cadillac and take him home.

Ray Wiltsie (hired August 25, 1920) was an extra board engineer from Oswego. He was another Depression-era fireman who suffered through many layoffs during that time. Living in Oswego was one advantage, as he would fire steam-powered lake boats while furloughed. Wiltsie demonstrated his mechanical expertise on an Alco RS-3, working a peddler freight. The ratchet on the throttle handle was making any movement difficult. Taking the cab broom handle, Ray sliced a sliver off and, using his pliers, inserted it disengaging the ratchet. Sudden bursts of power during flat switching was exhilarating.

Winter weather on the division could be difficult, especially under blizzard conditions. Wiltsie was handling No. 337, a Syracuse/Oswego, passenger local, with poor visibility. Wiltsie stepped up the speed on a tangent portion of the track north of Woodard. Before he knew it, he was into the 25 mph curve approaching the bridge at Three Rivers. It was touch and go for a few seconds, but his engine and train made it around safely. While stopped in Phoenix, his conductor walked up to the engine, telling him that a few Pullman passengers got rolled around in their berths.

Another winter incident had Wiltsie involved in a train/auto collision on an unplowed crossing. Headlight and horn blowing did not deter the motorist. Radios on equipment was unheard of in early diesel times, so medical emergencies could be lengthy in waiting for an ambulance to arrive. As the motorist victim was somewhat ambulatory, Wiltsie moved him to the locomotive cab to keep him from freezing. Moral of the story: the patient survived and sued the railroad!

Bob "Slugger" Dowie (hired September 24, 1925) was another Oswego engineer with a great personality that was interesting to watch when running engines. Dowie lost four fingers of his right hand in a boiler accident years back. He was given the moniker by some cruel soul but never let it bother him. Any steam locomotive Dowie fired was distinctive, as he would take a knife and carve the handle of the scoop so he could wrap his thumb around it. He was a little man and sometimes used a cushion on his seat to make it easier to reach the controls. There was a certain freight yard that had a good restaurant across the street Dowie liked to go to. On our way to it, Dowie would reach in the pocket of his frock, pulling out his false teeth. Snapping them in place, he would remark, "Gotta look good for the waitresses."

Joe Lane (hired May 10, 1941) was the second fireman hired in 1941. With World War II looming, traffic was picking up, and the extra boards were busy handling additional trains. Lane's sense of humor got him around several of the division's detractors that firemen hated. Promotional exams for the right-hand seat box were encouraged. Within a couple of years, he would be called as an extra board engineer.

One of his first trips was running No. 80, the southbound passenger train from Ogdensburg. Boarding the engine at Watertown, the assigned F-12 ten-wheeler handled the train beautifully at 55 mph. Descending the long grade to Utica, there was suddenly a battering of the floorboard on the fireman's side of the engine. Lane put the brakes into emergency as he theorized a side rod had broken. A whirling side rod could easily dig into the roadbed, causing a derailment. His theory was correct, and he safely stopped the train. His fireman was so traumatized from the event that he passed away the following week.

The Utica depot switcher was another St. Lawrence job. Joe was firing it one day when a road foreman of engines came running down the platform, hollering for Lane to pick up his grip and get off the engine. Leading him over to another platform, he told him to board an eastbound passenger engine going to Albany. The fireman had taken sick and gotten off. Lane examined the fire after boarding. Getting the stoker into action and distributing the coal evenly, he got the steam pressure back up to normal. He sat back for the remainder of the trip, enjoying the Mohawk Valley scenery.

At Albany, another surprise was in store. The Hudson Division fireman did not show up, and another road foreman instructed Joe to stay aboard to Harmon. It became a long day for Joe, but the real pleasure was firing one of the new Niagaras, capable of sustained running at 100 mph.

Joe Lane's other memorable trip with steam came with a little unplanned humor thrown in. He and another 1941 fireman, Jack Carnes, were called for a troop train movement from Syracuse to Fort Drum north of Watertown. They picked up their train at the Syracuse depot. Motive power was a mainline Mohawk, slightly under the Niagara in statistics but more than capable for the job. Taking the train to its destination, they were issued orders to return light to Syracuse. At Pulaski, they were handed up orders to meet and assist No. 336 at Woodard, the passenger train from Oswego. Its motive power was a former B&A commuter engine that was having steaming problems. Coupling onto the train, they discovered the engineer was the chief tormentor when Lane and Carnes were rookie firemen. Lane hollered to Carnes, "Get up a head of steam, as we're going to give that SOB a ride." Ride they did, passing the south switch at 65 and rolling through Liverpool at 73 mph. Looking back at his adversary, the old guy was gripping the brake stand with his left hand while his right hand was gripping the window armrest.

Joe, always the prankster, decided to have some fun with a senior engineer who would be a likely candidate. When the opportunity arose, Lane opened up the engine compartment door and isolated three of the six fuel injectors of the Alco S-2. With the engine coughing, wheezing, spitting, and belching white smoke, it continued to run even though erratically. Arriving at an engine facility, the engineer needed an explanation for the work report. Lane told him to put down "needs new spark plugs." The engineer would never set foot there again due to all the guffaws of the maintenance people.

Joe Lane had relatively harmless solutions to locomotive problems, although most unconventional. An annoying flat wheel on the truck beneath the cab of an Alco RS-3 got Lane's attention. In the back of his mind would be the perfect location to remedy the problem. The perfect location turned out to be a propane gas customer with a grade and S-curve coming back up to the main track. Pulling out a string of empty tankers and once into the curve, Lane advanced the throttle to full. Within a couple of seconds, the offending wheel went into a massive slip, with the speed recorder needle zipping up the dial to 40 mph. The brakemen riding the rear ladder were moving up to escape the flames coming off the wheels. Arriving on the main track, the flat wheel problem had been taken care of. The wheel lathe at DeWitt could not have done better.

Another troop movement from Syracuse northward proved interesting. Normally, mainline passenger diesels would be taken off as the grades of the division were challenging to their high-speed gear ratios. This trip had Alco FA cab units, as steam heat was unnecessary. Stopping on the passing siding at Adams, the troop sergeant came forward to ask Joe the reason for the delay. Then he asked for a cab ride, which Joe agreed to. To best describe the guy, he was a facsimile of Sarge in the *Beetle Bailey* comic strip. A high-speed ride down the grade into Watertown was thought-appropriate. It was not long before their "passenger" was not feeling too well, with all the rocking and swaying in the cab. A curve ahead preceding a blind crossing was blown for, as the needle was hovering around 98 mph. As the crossing swung into view, a gasoline tanker truck was poking across it. The frantic whistleblowing alerted the driver, and the rig was missed by only a few feet.

The troop sergeant had long since come alive with "we're going to get killed" and profanities when seeing the gasoline truck. When the train stopped at Massey Yard, he had enough and was still muttering things about the engine crew under his breath as he descended the engine ladder.

There was a freight job between Rome and Richland that used the mainline from Utica. Joe Lane liked it, as there was little work to be done Saturdays. The object of the exercise was to get back to Utica as soon as possible to catch a collegiate football game at a favorite watering hole. This particular Saturday was very snowy. As was the habit of St. Lawrence crews using track 4 of the mainline, 80 mph speeds were common. The 19000 series of old derelict but usable wooden cabooses were still being used. Lane was speeding along with his Alco RS-3 when, suddenly, he felt the brakes coming on. He realized that the conductor was using his brake valve in the caboose. Lane allowed the train to stop and waited it out for an explanation from the rear of the train. Thirty minutes later, the rear brakeman appeared. He responded, "Well, it's kinda like this. There was a blizzard going on inside the caboose." The conductor was rewarded with the moniker "Brake Valve."

There was a switching job on the north side of Syracuse requiring some street running. Trains competing with automobiles on a street is a recipe for disaster unless each party is careful. While steam power was still around in 1951, a U-3 switcher was backing a string of cars down the street. Engine and train crew were strategically spotted to make this a safe move. With all eyes focused in the direction of the move, an incident had occurred unnoticed. A wrap-around bumper on a brand new Buick parked too close had snagged the yoke of the valve gear on the engine. Reluctantly dragged along for several hundred feet before being discovered, it must have been quite a surprise to everyone—as well as the car's owner!

Another legendary story on the division everyone talked about was a mixed train on the north end operated by a senior crew with accumulated service totaling 175 years. Naturally, they acquired habits working with each other that could be rib-tickling. The conductor wore a dress shirt and tie under his bib overalls and high-top shoes. He always carried the latest employee timetable folded in his back pocket. One day, the baggage man told him that a delivery was to be made at a depot along their route. The conductor became very angry about the depot not being a scheduled stop, and the train would not make an exception.

Undaunted, the baggage man dropped a message off at the station preceding where the delivery would be made. He instructed the operator to relay instructions that the delivery would be found in the pond beyond the depot. When the train reached the delivery point, the baggage man opened the baggage door as the train crossed the pond on a trestle. Leading a young heifer to the open door, he swatted it on the rear, causing it to bolt out of the car and land in the pond with a spectacular splash.

It was during this period of time that freight crews numbered seven individuals so that various switching tasks could be accomplished. Each trainman was responsible for his part in the maneuver. Quite frequently, it was necessary to get a freight car or more from behind the locomotive ahead of it, requiring a move known to railroaders as a "flying switch" or "drop." Where there was a facing point track switch to a siding or other track and there was ample room for a rolling car(s), a coordinated effort of the train crew could accomplish the task.

The background to this eyewitness event occurred in the early 1950s when eleven 65-foot gondolas were picked up by a crew. They had been unloaded beforehand, but the engine was on the wrong end of them to be put in the train. The conductor rehearsed the brakemen in what needed to be done, with one to man the switch, one to uncouple the cars from the engine, and one to ride the last gondola manning the handbrake. Fortunately, there was a slight downhill grade to keep the cars rolling at a moderate speed.

Once backed up 1,000 feet from the switch, the engine started ahead at a high rate of speed, releasing the cars a good 500 feet from the switch and continued to race onto the siding. As soon as the engine cleared, the switch was thrown over to the main track as the cars sped through. What was amusing was because of the speed of the cars, the brakeman manning the handbrake had his frock perfectly horizontal behind him—he looked like Superman.

This type of switching move became commonplace on the railroad and even on occasion involved the engine crew trading places with the others.

Jimmy "Boy Wonder" Hart (hired August 18, 1917) was another great personality. Known to all of his division as well as neighboring divisions, he was interesting to watch operating locomotives. The steel suitcase he carried was another item to see inside. Besides his personal effects, he carried large wrenches, a ball-peen hammer, and specially made extension handles for engine controls that might require a long reach to operate. Hart was another that would not be blamed for an engine failure out on the road. The amusing part of the suitcase was at the end of a run leaving the locomotive. The usual formality was for the fireman to go down the ladder first. The engineer would then drop the suitcases to him to catch. One can only imagine a hapless fireman catching Jimmy's 50-pound suitcase.

My first locomotive picture was given to me by Jimmy. It showed him in the fireman's seat of an I-class 4-4-2, taken at Wilson, New York, in the 1930s, before those locomotives were retired. Asking him about speed on that section of the railroad, he calmly mentioned 85 mph on certain occasions. With towns being so close to each other as well as village ordinances for train speed in each, there must have been some wild rides. Hart had a large family at home, and whenever he was at a terminal, he would be asked by a number of trainmen how many kids he had. His usual reply was, "Last time I left the house, there were six, maybe another when I get back!"

Jimmy Hart probably held the distinction of operating the last revenue steam power on the St. Lawrence Division. Interestingly enough, it was not a New York Central engine. The occasion was a 1954 Syracuse Historical Society excursion going to Lacona, New York. The locomotive was No. 38, a former Huntington & Broad Top 2-8-0 that had been brought up from southern Pennsylvania. It had been purchased for the Rail City Museum, close to Lacona, on the shore of Lake Ontario. Pulling a string of coaches, it closed the door on steam for the division. Jimmy's son Davey, a fireman, was the other engine crew member.

GEORGE "DOGGY DADDY" SCHARF (HIRED JULY 20, 1923) had a son ROBERT ("AUGGIE DOGGIE"), a fireman. How these monikers were awarded was anyone's guess. George dated back to early days, when he fired for Harry Doonan. He was careful and exact in all of his locomotive operations. A true gentleman, he was a pleasure to be around and a true credit to his profession. He had one unpleasant event when working a snowplow extra near Woodard. When charging an enormous snowdrift with his pair of Alco FAs, the plow overturned into a ditch, pulling the engines with it. George suffered a broken leg in the accident. Hard-packed snow could lift equipment off the rails and cause a derailment..

A never-to-be-repeated diesel operation involved George Scharf running DFO-1 in April 1960 on the Phoenix branch. A strange horn blowing aroused my curiosity as two Alco PA cab units headed up the train. Not wanting to miss a second look, I traveled north to watch them assault the Great Bear Hill near Fulton. Six-wheel trucks on passenger road locomotives running over an 80-pound rail seemed as strange as a Rolls Royce showing up in my living room. Watching them smoking their way up the grade, Scharf recognized me from a distance and was patting the side of the lead unit as he came by.

The units were subsidiary Pittsburg & Lake Erie engines. As I would later learn, the units had just been outshopped at DeWitt, having their boilers removed and regeared for freight service. The NYC's PAs were also modified, as these units still had road service time left before eventual retirement. The railroad was also in a financial crunch, and rebuilt power was important.

Then there was the unusual Sunday afternoon phone call to an enginehouse from a distant point where a freight crew was ready to start their run. The report was made that the bell on the locomotive was not working; it was serious stuff for a locomotive not to have an operating bell. The locomotive inspector on duty decided to drive over to ascertain the difficulty. Arriving, he gave a cursory examination and then quizzed the crew. Asking whether they had examined the bell, their reply was negative. He then announced there was *no* bell, as it was stolen. Located behind the pilot, it was probably an easy heist.

Probably my favorite engineer was **EDDIE COLLINS (HIRED AUGUST 18, 1916)** from Oswego. Collins was not only a great engineer, but also a real humanitarian He represented his Catholic faith in his work and great tolerance to his detractors. He was a pleasure to watch, handling long trains or yard jobs. He announced to me one night he was bidding on a yard job closer to home and probably would not be seeing me again. As I was leaving his engine, he offered words of encouragement to my future that had never been said before. I tried to keep back tears in my eyes. That was Eddie Collins and the way he'll always be. Fortunately, I encountered him on his other job one afternoon, which would be my last. It was shortly after that I learned of his passing.

My last comical friend and a true legend of the St. Lawrence Division was **Louis Beeman (hired September 25, 1945).** To give the reader a little understanding of the story, the window-lowering handle on the Alco cab units must be described. Quite unique from the other makes, it had a long, straight handle below the window that accomplished everything with just a nudge in either direction. Adjacent to it was another small handle of the same shape that was the acknowledging lever for the automatic train stop. This handle had to be pulled to acknowledge any restrictive signal in train control territory. Failure would result in the train brakes going into emergency.

Louis was firing for John "Smiling Jack" Bragger on WD-2 during an after-dark, heavy snowstorm. The day had been long for both, and Beeman had taken over the engineer's seat for the remainder of the trip. They were probably in a daze with the headlight against the blowing snow as the signal at SS-JG suddenly appeared. Beeman made a dive for the ATS handle, the window came down, and the brakes went on.

Embarrassed by his blunder as soon as the train stopped, he opened the cab door and descended the ladder to hit the reset button under the car body. Expecting to hit the ground, he suddenly tumbled about 10 feet into an industrial creek. His engine had stopped on a deck girder bridge. Luckily unhurt, he wasted no time in getting out of the freezing water and back on the engine. Bragger bellowed, "Where have you been? Why are you all wet? Go back in the cab of the trailing unit because you stink."

The division went into hysterics as the news about Louis quickly circulated. In mere hours, dirty engines had scrawlings that read, "This engine washed at Beeman's Beech," and on depots, written in chalk, were such things as "13.6 miles to Beeman's Beach–Dive in with Louis." Thus the legend lasted for many years. Beeman must have loved it, as he was that type of railroader.

Eight

Seniority Rosters

Included for reader enjoyent are the seniority rosters for operating employees during this period. Possibly, a family member who worked for the railroad division might be found. Dates of hiring and any promotion are indicated. Despite layoffs and service in world conflicts, seniority dates remained intact thanks to labor contracts protecting members.

THE NEW YORK CENTRAL RAILROAD COMPANY

SENIORITY ROSTER

for

ENGINEMEN & FIREMEN

ST LAWRENCE DIVISION

January 1 1948

Seniority Dates of Enginemen and Firemen
St. Lawrence Division
January 1 1948

DP - Disability Pension # - Military Service

				Fireman	Engineman
1	P	Pettis	G. N.	Dec 13 1899	Jan 17 1904
2		Halpin	T. F.	Sep 13 1899	Feb 9 1904
3		Searow	J.	Jan 20 1902	Oct 10 1905
4		Hourigan	F. J.	Jul 21 1902	Feb 12 1906
5		Smith	F. H.	Jul 26 1902	Feb 13 1906
6		Callentine	A.	Sep 15 1902	Feb 19 1906
7	P	Fanning	W. C.	Feb 7 1903	Jan 8 1907
8		Mahaney	E. D.	Jun 13 1903	Jan 13 1907
9	P	Bartelson	S. J.	Jun 21 1903	Jan 14 1907
10	P	McNamara	F. J.	Jul 6 1903	Jan 16 1907
11	P	Simonds	O.	Nov 3 1903	Oct 5 1907
12		Baker	G. G.	Jan 17 1904	Oct 20 1907
13	P	Robinson	R.	Dec 3 1907	Dec 8 1907
14		Donovan	D. C.	Feb 10 1904	Dec 19 1907
15		Ciblin	C. P.	Mar 4 1904	Feb 1 1908
16		Madden	F. W.	Apr 11 1904	Feb 22 1908
17		Smith	F. R.	Jul 15 1904	Dec 3 1908
18		Kelly	C. H.	Oct 22 1904	Dec 5 1908
19		Aldridge	W. F.	Nov 2 1904	Dec 6 1908
20		Gurley	C. N.	Dec 3 1904	Dec 9 1908
21	P	Sherwood	M.	Dec 11 1904	Dec 11 1908
22	P	Robinson	M. T.	Dec 24 1904	Dec 14 1908
23	P	Catlin	A. C.	Dec 26 1904	Dec 16 1908
24	P	Cauley	J. F.	Feb 5 1905	Jan 16 1909
25	Yd	Ocllins	D.J.	Sep 10 1905	Jan 18 1909
26		Sherwood	L. R.	Sep 13 1905	Jan 20 1909
27		Haley	M.	Aug 20 1905	Nov 22 1909
28	P	Feeley	J. J.	Dec 17 1905	Nov 25 1909
29		Donovan	L. R.	Dec 30 1905	Dec 1 1909
30	P	Stone	W. R.	Jul 30 1906	Jun 16 1910
31	P	Neville	F.	Aug 2 1906	Jun 17 1910
32		Albert	H. M.	Aug 31 1906	Jun 20 1910
33	P	Lamb	G.	Sep 2 1906	Aug 3 1911
34	P	Handricks	W. P.	Oct 7 1905	Aug 19 1911
35	P	Mowers	A. M.	Feb 25 1906	Nov 1 1912
36	P	Parody	G. H.	Sep 3 1906	Nov 2 1912
37	P	Tuell	C. O.	Sep 30 1906	Nov 3 1912
38	P	Thiebeau	J. B.	Oct 24 1906	Nov 7 1912
39	P	Doonan	H. N.	Nov 14 1906	Nov 9 1912
40	P	Peavey	W. E.	Jan 4 1907	Nov 13 1912
41	P	Mack	C. J.	Jan 14 1907	Nov 17 1912
42	P	Murphy	F. J.	Jan 16 1907	Nov 18 1912
43	P	Severance	A. F.	Jan 18 1907	Nov 19 1912
44		Dermady	F.V.	Jan 21 1907	Nov 20 1912
45	P	Weyeneth	R. E.	Jan 28 1907	Nov 24 1912

46	YD	Connors	L.	Feb 12 1907	---------
47		Donaldson	S. R.	Jun 2 1907	Jan 19 1913
48	P	Laventure	G.	Jun 23 1907	Jan 19 1913
49	P	Moore	R. W.	Jun 28 1907	Jan 21 1913
50	P	Kinsella	J. A.	Jul 19 1907	Jan 25 1913
51	P	Parry	R. J.	Aug 3 1907	Jan 26 1913
52	Yd	Thompson	H.R.	Aug 12 1907	Jan 29 1913
53	P	Worden	H. J.	Oct 19 1907	Jan 31 1913
54	P	Major	H. J.	Jan 3 1908	Jan 31 1913
55		Blake	C. J.	Jan 8 1908	Feb 3 1913
56		Terrott	J. P.	Mar 10 1908	Feb 6 1913
57		Soper	J. H.	Jul 9 1908	Feb 7 1913
58	P	Lee	T. M.	Aug 21 1908	Feb 8 1913
59		Galvin	E. D.	Sep 3 1908	Feb 9 1913
60	P	Grimshaw	H. G.	Sep 16 1908	Feb 12 1913
61		Millard	F. T.	Jun 23 1909	Feb 15 1913
62		Buckingham	H. A.	Jul 2 1909	Feb 17 1913
63	P	Murdock	D. A. G.	Jul 2 1909	Feb 18 1913
64	P	Shoultz	H. I.	Jal 15 1909	Feb 20 1913
65		Fuller	F. L.	Oct 3 1909	Apr 1 1913
66	P	McCarthy	A. J.	Oct 7 1909	Apr 2 1913
67	P	Moulton	O. L.	Oct 24 1909	Apr 6 1913
68	YD	Thompson	H. C.	Jan 7 1910	Apr 12 1913
69	P	Outhbertson	O. H.	Jan 8 1910	Apr 14 1913
70	P	Jensen	J. A.	Jan 13 1910	Jan 1 1913
71		Palmer	B. H.	Jan 21 1910	Jun 12 1913
72	P	Alexander	G.C.	Mar 30 1910	Jun 22 1913
73	P	Downey	C.	Aug 14 1910	Jun 27 1913
74	P	Dimmeck	C. S.	Aug 15 1910	Jun 28 1913
75		Lewis	H. J.	Aug 21 1910	Jun 29 1913
76		Kellison	W.	Jan 2 1911	Jul 15 1913
77	P	McGraw	J. F.	Jul 10 1911	Jul 20 1913
78		Barber	H. C.	Jul 22 1911	Jul 23 1913
79		Budd	G. F.	Jul 25 1911	Sep 21 1913
80		Bristol	C. A.	Aug 14 1911	Jun 3 1918
81		Spath	J. J.	Aug 14 1911	Jun 5 1918
82	YD	Robinson	W. P.	Sep 4 1911	Jun 6 1918
83	P	Hockey	R. E.	Sep 18 1911	Jun 7 1918
84		Kapfer	W. H.	Oct 1 1911	Jun 8 1918
85	P	Freeman	B. J.	Nov 14 1911	Jun 10 1918
86	P	Smith	D. A.	Nov 22 1911	Jun 11 1918
87	P	Wells	D. A.	Feb 18 1912	Jun 14 1918
88	P	Quinn	C. J.	Aug 6 1912	Jun 15 1918
89	YD	Bearden	F.	Aug 22 1912	---------
90		Wanck	A.	Aug 25 1912	Jun 17 1918
91		McGraw	R. H.	Sep 11 1912	Jun 19 1918
92		Langouer	D. J.	Sep 23 1912	Sep 25 1918
93		Green	G. W.	Oct 24 1911	Sep 27 1918
94		Mallett	D. J.	Jan 20 1913	Sep 28 1918
95	P	Sanderl	R. P.	Apr 14 1913	Sep 29 1918
96		Alexander	W. F.	Jun 22 1913	Sep 30 1918
97	P	Peggs	J. B.	Aug 2 1913	Oct 4 1918
98	YD	Doan	E. W.	May 3 1916	Aug 23 1919
99		Collins	E. F.	Aug 18 1916	Sep 25 1919
100		Bragger	J. T.	Aug 20 1916	Oct 25 1919

101		Collins	T.	Aug 22 1916	Sep 23 1920
102		Manchester	R. D.	Aug 25 1916	Sep 30 1920
103	H	Forsyth	W. H.	Sep 4 1916	-------
104	P	Reynolds	E. L.	Jan 6 1917	May 9 1921
105	P	McDonald	J. V.	Jan 20 1917	Aug 23 1922
106		Kendrew	R.	Jan 28 1917	Aug 30 1922
107	P	Terry	G. D.	Feb 1 1917	Sep 23 1922
108	P	Barry	H. P.	Feb 2 1917	Oct 12 1922
109		Peterson	A. V.	Feb 28 1917	May 1 1923
110	P	Bristol	W. P.	Mar 7 1917	Jun 1 1923
111	P	Corey	B. C.	Mar 15 1917	Jul 1 1923
112	P	Worden	H. M.	Mar 16 1917	Aug 1 1923
113	P	Reilly	T. P.	May 1 1917	Aug 20 1923
114	YD	Tewksbury	T. G.	Jun 1 1917	Aug 25 1923
115	YD	Easter	J. R.	Jun 15 1917	-------
116		Curtis	H. G.	Jul 7 1917	Sep 1 1923
117	P	Sandle	F. B.	Jul 8 1917	Sep 3 1923
118	P	Isham	S.	Jul 23 1917	Sep 7 1923
119		Palmer	J. M.	Jul 26 1917	Sep 8 1923
120	YD	Dillabough	G. L.	Aug 3 1917	-------
121	P	Ward	C. M.	Aug 6 1917	Oct 2 1923
122	P	Cataldo	J.	Aug 6 1917	Oct 10 1923
123	P	Ward	D. E.	Aug 11 1917	Jun 10 1924
124	P	Hart	J. D.	Aug 18 1917	Jul 10 1924
125	P	Vautrin	M. R.	Aug 22 1917	Jul 20 1924
126	P	Stephens	J. F.	Aug 31 1917	Aug 15 1924
127		Cushing	A. J.	Sep 1 1917	Aug 16 1924
128	P	Whitcomb	G. W.	Sep 3 1917	Aug 16 1924
129	P	Morris	G. T.	Sep 15 1917	Aug 18 1924
130	P	Warner	H.	Oct 14 1917	Aug 22 1924
131		Ball	L. A.	Nov 4 1917	Aug 24 1924
132	P	Pierre	E. G.	Mar 23 1918	Aug 26 1924
133		Widrig	J. E.	Jun 8 1918	Aug 26 1924
134	P	Healy	J. L.	Jul 2 1918	Aug 27 1924
135	YD	Siegel	M. J.	Sep 7 1918	-----
136		Ruestow	C. C.	Oct 15 1918	Aug 30 1924
137		Davenport	A. C.	Oct 26 1918	Sep 5 1924
138	P	King	M. G.	Nov 20 1918	Sep 10 1924
139	P	Stark	L. W.	Nov 21 1918	Sep 30 1924
140		Capron	C. E.	Jan 5 1920	Jun 1 1925
141	P	Dunn	C. E.	Jan 18 1920	Jun 2 1925
142	YD	Augustus	J. E.	Jan 21 1920	-------
143		Richardson	R. H.	Jan 23 1920	Jun 5 1925
144	P	Burningham	C. J.	Jan 27 1920	Jun 7 1925
145		Hayes	T. W.	Feb 12 1920	Oct 21 1942
146		Scheel	E. W.	Feb 15 1920	Oct 22 1942
147		Kellogg	J. B.	Feb 24 1920	Oct 23 1942
148	P	Foley	J. D.	Mar 1 1920	Oct 24 1942
149		Loveland	L. A.	Mar 7 1920	Oct 25 1942
150		Reynolds	S. R.	Mar 8 1920	Oct 26 1942
151	YD	Putnam	E.	Mar 21 1920	Oct 27 1942
152		Barker	C. H.	Jul 11 1920	Oct 28 1942
153		Lobdell	H. V.	Aug 7 1920	Oct 29 1942
154		Wiltsie	R. M.	Aug 25 1920	Oct 30 1942
155		LaValla	J. W.	Aug 25 1920	Oct 30 1942

156		McClelland	H.	Sep 1 1920	Nov 1 1942
157		Dulmage	W. C.	Sep 1 1920	Nov 2 1942
158		Waterbury	E. L.	Sep 7 1920	Nov 3 1942
159		Briglin	F. A.	Sep 7 1920	Nov 4 1942
160	YD	Fricke	W. H.	Sep 10 1920	-------
161		Peck	E. G.	Sep 15 1920	Nov 6 1942
162		Lacy	F. E.	Sep 24 1920	Nov 7 1942
163		Doule	A. J.	Oct 10 1920	Nov 8 1942
164		Maine	M. R.	Oct 20 1920	Nov 9 1942
165	P	Bailey	W. B.	Dec 1 1920	Nov 10 1942
166		Kelly	J. E.	Dec 9 1920	Nov 11 1942
167		Morden	E. T.	Dec 13 1920	Nov 13 1942
168	YD	Planty	W. G.	Dec 20 1920	Nov 13 1942
169		Munson	H. S.	Dec 28 1920	Nov 14 1942
170		Farnsworth	A. L.	Nov 18 1922	Nov 15 1942
171		Kaine	J. A.	Jan 25 1923	Nov 16 1942
172		Dyer	G. W.	Feb 13 1923	Nov 17 1942
173		Neilsen	H. P.	Feb 27 1923	Nov 9 1945
174		Halpin	R. D.	Jul 13 1923	Nov 10 1945
175		Wolfe	W. H.	Jul 19 1923	Nov 11 1945
176		Scharf	G. F.	Jul 20 1923	Nov 12 1945
177		Groth	G. W.	Aug 22 1923	Nov 13 1945
178		Warsop	C.	Sep 6 1923	Nov 14 1945
179		Dowie	R. J.	Sep 24 1925	Nov 15 1945
180		Flack	W. M.	Jan 30 1926	Nov 16 1945
181		Charlebois	V. J.	Mar 1 1926	Nov 17 1945
182		Langouer	B. J.	Mar 6 1926	Nov 18 1945
183		Mooney	C.	Sep 30 1926	Nov 19 1945
184		Brown	R.	Dec 10 1926	Nov 20 1945
185		Horth	L. R.	Dec 23 1926	Nov 21 1945
186		Wright	H. S.	Jan 1 1927	Nov 22 1945
187		Phelps	G. E.	Jan 23 1927	Nov 23 1945
188		Parrott	H. F.	Sep 2 1928	Nov 24 1945
189		Fleming	E. M.	Aug 20 1929	Nov 25 1945
190		Hardy	R. J.	Jan 19 1940	Nov 26 1945
191		Maville	B. L.	Dec 4 1940	Jun 16 1947
192		Palmer	C. M.	Apr 4 1941	
193		Lane	J. D.	May 10 1941	
194		DeFresne	P. A.	May 31 1941	
195		Spaziani	S. J.	Jun 2 1941	
196		Mangini	A. A.	Jun 2 1941	
197		Bickel	G. R.	Jun 28 1941	
198		Martin	G. E.	Jul 2 1941	
199		Watson	G. L.	Jul 4 1941	
200		Robarge	D. F.	Jul 25 1941	
201		Lowe	K. M.	Jul 27 1941	
202		Baxter	R. M.	Jul 30 1941	
203		Kelly	K. W.	Aug 1 1941	
204		Cozzie	R. C.	Aug 1 1941	
205		Lake	P. A.	Aug 6 1941	
206		Cosselman	K.	Aug 9 1941	
207		Macauley	E. S.	Aug 9 1941	
208		Sovie	J. J.	Aug 13 1941	
209		Lingenfelter	L. S.	Aug 13 1941	
210		Sullivan	E. P.	Aug 22 1941	

211		Wart	R. E.	Aug 25 1941
212		Ball	E. M.	Aug 26 1941
213		Flack	L. W.	Aug 28 1941
214		Stark	E. W.	Aug 29 1941
215		Newcomb	A. D.	Aug 29 1941
216		Ashwin	N. W.	Aug 29 1941
217		Ward	T. W.	Sep 15 1941
218		Carnes	J. H.	Sep 18 1941
219		Devine	W. T.	Sep 26 1941
220		Kavanaugh	J. F.	Nov 6 1941
221		Bartelson	J. S.	Nov 25 1941
222		Cerow	R. W.	Dec 2 1941
223		Burke	R. E.	Dec 10 1941
224		Godfrey	L. P.	Dec 12 1941
225		Stone	T. M.	Jan 28 1942
226		Rose	G. C.	Jul 20 1942
227		Khammar	F. A.	Jul 8 1942
228		Frasher	E. P.	Jul 18 1942
229		Mitchell	S. M.	Jul 24 1942
230		Sturtz	G. S.	Jul 28 1942
231		White	J. L.	Aug 1 1942
232		Thenell	L. E.	Aug 14 1942
233		Payne	N.R.	Aug 22 1942
234		McCarthy	C. T.	Sep 1 1942
235		O'Brien	J. T.	Sep 2 1942
236		Finley	T. C.	Sep 9 1942
237		Fox	W. L.	Sep 12 1942
238		Duflo	S. J.	Oct 9 1942
239		Cirrincione	F. J.	Oct 29 1942
240		Malcolm	M. K.	Dec 30 1942
241		Lee	A. G.	Jan 12 1943
242		Mothersell	W. G.	Jan 13 1943
243		Stubbs	R. W.	Jan 21 1943
244	H	Ellis	H. B.	Jan 28 1943
245		Stevens	G. D.	Feb 3 1943
246		Hollis	L. W.	Feb 6 1943
247		Verne	H. A.	Feb 8 1943
248		Bell	W. J. Jr.	Feb 9 1943
249		Hanlon	J. J.	Feb 9 1943
250		Fanser	L. C.	Feb 10 1943
251		Pecori	J. P.	Feb 18 1943
252		Dimmock	W. V.	Feb 18 1943
253		Ridgeway	L. M.	Feb 19 1943
254		Burnett	T. J.	Feb 21 1943
255		Bothwell	R. E.	Feb 26 1943
256		Pridgeon	R. Q.	Mar 3 1943
257		Dillabough	M. C.	Mar 7 1943
258		Charlebois	G. F.	Mar 30 1943
259		Jones	R. E.	Aug 11 1943
260		Delaney	P. A.	Aug 15 1943
261		Scharf	L. W.	Sep 12 1943
262		LaForest	J. R.	Sep 16 1943
263		Britton	L. G.	Oct 5 1943
264		Dorough	H. E.	Oct 8 1943
265		Martin	H.	Oct 14 1943

266		Hickey	J. J.	Oct 16 1943
267		Clow	L. E.	Oct 23 1943
268		Gilbert	G. A.	Dec 7 1943
269	H	Wright	C.	Dec 17 1943
270	H	Dufore	J. A.	Dec 17 1943
271		Scanlon	T. E.	Jan 4 1944
272		Kehoe	L. A.	Jan 16 1944
273		Babbitt	R. A.	Jan 18 1944
274		McCormick	C. J.	Mar 28 1944
275		Weir	L. L.	May 3 1944
276		Purvis	F. W.	Jul 10 1944
277		Altmire	D. F.	Sep 15 1944
278		Howard	N. W.	Oct 31 1944
279		Wagoner	C. E.	Nov 9 1944
280		Whattam	J. A.	Jan 13 1945
281		Tiff	O. W.	Jan 18 1945
282		Redmond	L. M.	Mar 16 1945
283		Hoey	S. J.	Apr 5 1945
284		Dompiere	W. A.	Apr 6 1945
285		Ives	K. F.	Jul 8 1945
286		Bilby	J. R.	Sep 25 1945
287		Beeman	L. J.	Sep 25 1945
288		Oliver	W. W.	Oct 1 1945
289		O'Riley	H. G.	Oct 14 1945
290		Miles	A. L.	Nov 26 1945
291		Dudeck	V. M.	Dec 7 1945
292	#	O'Brien	W. E.	Dec 15 1945
293		Horton	P. E.	Dec 20 1945
294		Shepard	H. E.	Dec 20 1945
295		Andrews	E. J.	Dec 1945
296		Balletine	D. W.	Jan 1945
297		Flitcroft	J. B.	Jan 1945
298		Maitland	J. C.	Feb 1945
299		Claney	J. E.	Oct 1945
300		Sprague	R. L.	1947
301		Foster	R. C.	1947
302		Williams	M. R.	1947
303		Bickel	C. L.	1947
304		Blevins	L. J.	1947
305		Hart	D. J.	1947
306		Burnell	F. E.	1947
307		Porter	E. S.	1947
308		Collins	G. F.	1947
309		Robinson	V. C.	1947
310		Dorrough	C. E.	1947
311		Ramsay	B. L.	1947
312		Cummings	J. E.	1947
313		Ball	K. H.	1947
314		Cook	C. D.	1947
315		Covey	R.	1947
316		Goff	E. A.	1947
317		Halpin	M. H.	1947
318		Jenkins	R. E.	1947
319		Durant	C. L.	1947
320		King	C. T.	1947

321	McGregor	D. J.	1947
322	Dean	C.	1947
323	Johnson	H. F.	1947
324	Pettapiece	W. R.	1947
325	Frantz	R. L.	1947
326	Sansevere	A. P.	1947
327	McCarthy	J. T.	1947
328	Quinn	C. J.	1947
329	Branagan	W. W.	1947
330	Donovan	J. T.	1947
331	Donahue	B. T.	1947
332	Murray	H. F.	1947
333	Laboeuf	E. V.	1947
334	Davis	J. L.	1947
335	Jareo	L. W.	1947
336	Champagne	J. F.	1947
337	Newvine	G. A.	1947
338	Whalahan	W. H.	1947
339	Giddings	E. L.	1947
340	Slover	G. A.	1947

THE NEW YORK CENTRAL SYSTEM

SENIORITY ROSTER

TRAIN CREWS

ST LAWRENCE DIVISION

January 1 1955

Seniority Dates of Train Crew
St. Lawrence Division
January 1 1955

DP - Disability Pension   # - Military Service

			Brakeman	Freight Conductor	Passenger Conductor
1	Ladue	A. H.	Oct 4 1905	Sep 16 1907	Feb 5 1928
2	Dormady	S. L.	Sep 15 1906	Aug 20 1911	Apr 9 1930
3	Wilkins	A. R.	Mar 1 1907	Sep 12 1911	
4	Cross	G. D.	Apr 24 1907	Jun 8 1918	
5	Savage	R. F.	May 23 1907	Jun 11 1918	
6	Bechtle	C. E.	Jul 9 1907	Aug 9 1919	
7	Randall	E. E.	Feb 26 1908	Jan 4 1921	Dec 25 1940
8	Driscoll	D. F.	Oct 10 1908	Jan 9 1921	
9	Danzig	C. H.	Jul 29 1909	Jan 14 1921	
10	Jeffrey	J. E.	Nov 1 1909	Jan 16 1921	Jan 30 1942
11	Rainboth	C. F.	Nov 26 1909	Jan 17 1921	Jan 31 1942
12	Howard	W. M.	Jul 12 1910	Jan 21 1921	
13	Keene	W. H.	Jul 20 1910	Jan 22 1921	Feb 3 1942
14	Pelotte	A. J.	Jul 22 1910	Jan 22 1921	Feb 4 1942
15	English	W.	Jul 27 1910	Jan 24 1921	Feb 5 1942
16	Sullivan	G. C.	Aug 10 1910	Jan 27 1921	Feb 7 1942
17	Cardinal	E. F.	Jul 24 1911	Jul 4 1923	Feb 9 1942
18	Desens	A. J.	Jul 31 1911	Jul 5 1923	
19	McDonald	W. M.	Aug 25 1911	Jul 6 1923	Nov 4 1942
20	Brown	O. J.	Oct 19 1911	Jul 9 1923	
21	Thornhill	D. W.	Feb 10 1912	Jul 12 1923	
22	Carroll	L. J.	Sep 19 1912	Jul 20 1923	Nov 8 1942
23	McCormick	J. R.	Nov 15 1912	Jul 23 1923	
24	Carroll	J. H.	Mar 25 1913	Jul 26 1923	Nov 9 1942
25	Hooper	F. J.	Jul 3 1913	Jul 28 1923	
26 DP	O'Leary	J. D.	Jul 4 1913	Jul 31 1923	
27	Emlaw	F. N.	Aug 25 1913	Aug 6 1923	Nov 12 1942
28	Reifke	O.	Aug 27 1913		
29	Day	H. R.	Sep 6 1913		
30	Minkler	C. E.	Oct 8 1913	May 8 1930	Nov 16 1942
31	Lamora	G. W.	Mar 2 1916	May 9 1930	Nov 17 1942
32	Irvin	V. E.	Mar 3 1916	May 10 1930	Nov 18 1942
33	Macy	F. J.	Jun 18 1916		
34 DP	Cummings	P. L.	Jul 24 1916	May 14 1930	Nov 21 1942
35	Varley	J. W.	Aug 4 1916		
36	Widrig	W. D.	Aug 18 1916	Jan 28 1942	Nov 23 1945
37	Castle	W. D.	Aug 22 1916	Jan 29 1942	Nov 22 1942
38	Lock	C. W.	Aug 28 1916	Jan 30 1942	
39	Donahue	L. E.	Sep 18 1916	Jan 31 1942	Nov 23 1942
40	Baldwin	M.	Dec 30 1916		
41	Chapin	E. S.	Jan 5 1917	Feb 1 1942	Nov 24 1942
42	Lyindecker	G. A.	Jan 5 1917		
43	Stubbs	E. V.	Feb 27 1917	Feb 3 1942	
44	Franklin	H. F.	Mar 23 1917	Feb 4 1942	

45	Hughes	J. F.	Apr 3 1917	Feb 5 1942	Nov 26 1942
46	Gray	T. J.	Jun 14 1917	Feb 6 1942	Nov 27 1942
47	Rhouben	M. H.	Jul 17 1917	Feb 10 1942	Nov 24 1945
48	Fitzgibbons	E. A.	Jul 30 1917		
49	Duegaw	P. H.	Aug 24 1917	Feb 12 1942	Nov 26 1945
50	Babcock	J. C.	Oct 1 1917	Feb 14 1942	Nov 27 1945
51	Lago	A. B.	Oct 2 1917		
52	Chapin	R. H.	Oct 15 1917	Feb 15 1942	
53	Breese	H. H.	Apr 7 1918		
54	Payne	F.R.	Apr 12 1918	Feb 17 1942	
55	St. Pier	F.	Apr 26 1918		
56	Dempsey	W. M.	Aug 1 1918		
57	Proper	A. E.	Aug 2 1918	Feb 20 1942	Nov 28 1945
58	Sickelco	J. H.	Aug 24 1918	Feb 21 1942	
59	Phillips	E. P.	Oct 10 1918	Feb 22 1942	Nov 29 1945
60	Lake	D. C.	Oct 15 1918	Feb 23 1942	Nov 30 1945
61	Gray	W. F.	Oct 17 1918	Feb 24 1942	Jan 8 1946
62	Lewis	R.	Jul 12 1919	Nov 4 1942	Jan 11 1946
63	Talamo	A.	Aug 21 1919	Feb 25 1942	
64	Giblin	R. A.	Mar 4 1920	Feb 26 1942	Dec 2 1945
65	Graham	S. H.	Mar 18 1920	Feb 28 1942	Jan 10 1946
66	Holland	J. H.	Jul 1 1920	Mar 1 1942	
67 DP	DeGrasse	W. A.	Jul 12 1920		
68	Devine	J. B.	Jul 12 1920	Nov 5 1942	Jan 12 1946
69	Halstead	M. G.	Jul 19 1920	Nov 6 1942	Jan 13 1946
70	White	D. L.	Jul 20 1920	Nov 7 1942	Jan 14 1946
71	Gallegar	N. J.	Jul 23 1920	Nov 8 1942	Jan 15 1946
72	Donahue	C. O.	Jul 26 1920	Nov 9 1942	Jan 16 1946
73	Collins	J. H.	Aug 6 1920	Nov 10 1942	Aug 7 1947
74	Baker	C. J.	Aug 19 1920		
75	McMahon	F. J.	Sep 10 1920		
76	Vest	A. J.	Sep 20 1920	Nov 13 1942	Aug 8 1947
77	Mayne	L. R.	Sep 27 1920	Nov 15 1942	Aug 9 1947
78	Dishew	N. S.	Sep 29 1920		
79	Switzer	R. W.	Dec 4 1920		
80 DP	Lashor	A. A.	Dec 15 1920	Nov 16 1942	
81	Gray	J. A.	Dec 31 1920	Nov 17 1942	Aug 10 1947
82	White	C. E.	Dep 4 1922	Nov 18 1942	Aug 11 1947
83	Regan	C. F.	Dec 8 1922	Nov 19 1942	
84	Darlington	A. A.	Aug 15 1923		
85	Daly	E. F.	Aug 30 1923	Nov 20 1942	Aug 12 1947
86	Manchester	R. E.	Feb 16 1924	Nov 21 1942	
87	Familo	J.	Aug 27 1925	Nov 24 1942	Feb 12 1952
88	DuBois	L. F.	Aug 25 1926	Nov 25 1942	Feb 13 1952
89	Parker	E. S.	Aug 28 1926	Nov 26 1942	Aug 14 1947
90	Forbes	L. J.	Sep 16 1926		
91	Anable	L. J.	Oct 4 1926	Nov 27 1942	Aug 15 1947
92	Fletcher	A. A.	Dec 2 1926	Nov 28 1942	
93	Seaman	C. W.	Jul 21 1927	Nov 29 1942	
94	Rushlow	D. E.	Sep 5 1927	Nov 30 1942	Feb 14 1952
95	Grey	W. L.	Feb 13 1928	Dec 1 1942	Jul 13 1954
96	Fancher	E. R.	Sep 11 1928	Dec 1 1942	Feb 15 1952
97	Regan	D. J.	Oct 4 1928	Dec 2 1942	Feb 15 1952
98	Garrett	E. J.	Nov 19 1928	Dec 3 1942	
99	O'Neill	R. J.	Jan 23 1929	Mar 15 1946	Jul 14 1954

100	Munk	W. H.	Jun 25 1929		
101	Lynch	M. J.	Aug 21 1929	Dec 4 1942	Feb 16 1952
102 DP	Jareo	S. A.	Aug 26 1929		
103	Vout	W. H.	Sep 2 1929		
104	Bura	G. J.	Dec 29 1940	Mar 16 1946	Jul 15 1954
105	Ryan	H. K.	Jan 20 1941	Dec 6 1942	Feb 17 1952
106	Phillips	F. J.	Feb 8 1941	Mar 17 1946	
107	Hayes	H. E.	Mar 13 1941	Mar 18 1946	
108	Carson	W. A.	Apr 12 1941	Mar 19 1946	Feb 18 1952
109	Warner	E. R.	Apr 26 1941	Mar 20 1946	
110	Sigourney	J. C.	Apr 27 1941	Mar 22 1946	
111	Spangler	W. J.	May 4 1941	Mar 23 1946	
112	Brady	D. T.	May 17 1941	Mar 24 1946	Feb 21 1952
113	Gruenisen	E. W.	Jun 27 1941	Mar 25 1946	Jul 16 1954
114	Olah	J. J.	Jun 30 1941	Mar 26 1946	
115	Gebo	W. F.	Jul 12 1941	Mar 30 1946	
116	Strutz	D. A.	Jul 15 1941	Mar 31 1946	
117	St. Pierre	F. A.	Jul 16 1941		
118	Murphy	R. E.	Jul 21 1941	Apr 1 1946	
119	Lightfoot	J. W.	Aug 8 1941	Apr 3 1946	Feb 22 1952
120	Lightfoot	J. M.	Aug 8 1941	Oct 29 1946	Feb 24 1952
121	Kiah	C. F.	Aug 12 1941	Feb 13 1952	
122	Blake	E. J.	Aug 17 1941	Apr 6 1946	Feb 23 1952
123	Brockway	C. F.	Aug 20 1941	Apr 7 1946	Jul 17 1954
124	Gaudreau	H. P.	Aug 20 1941	Oct 30 1946	Jul 18 1954
125	Whitcomb	E. J.	Aug 28 1941	Feb 14 1952	Aug 9 1954
126	King	V. M.	Sep 2 1941	Nov 1 1946	Jul 19 1954
127	Lightholder	E. C.	Sep 2 1941	Nov 2 1946	Jul 20 1954
128	O'Conner	W. H.	Sep 5 1941	Nov 3 1946	Feb 25 1952
129	Oliver	J. A.	Sep 6 1941	Nov 5 1946	Feb 26 1952
130	Ryan	A. F.	Sep 7 1941	Nov 6 1946	Feb 27 1952
131	Downey	R. V.	Sep 7 1941	Nov 7 1946	
132	Moxley	T. J.	Sep 10 1941	Nov 8 1946	Jul 21 1954
133	Smith	H. A.	Sep 15 1941	Nov 9 1946	Jul 22 1954
134	Brouse	W. J.	Sep 19 1941	Nov 10 1946	Jul 23 1954
135	Silver	R. M.	Sep 20 1941	Nov 11 1946	Jul 24 1954
136	Chrissley	G. W.	Sep 20 1941	Nov 12 1946	Jul 25 1954
137	Franklin	Z. D.	Sep 25 1941	Nov 13 1946	Jul 26 1954
138	Orloff	J. A.	Oct 18 1941	Nov 16 1946	
139	King	E. J.	Oct 27 1941	Nov 17 1946	Jul 27 1954
140	Haskins	M. J.	Oct 28 1941		
141	Tully	J. T.	Oct 29 1941	Jan 5 1949	
142	Lincoln	D. J.	Oct 31 1941	Jan 6 1949	
143	Simser	H. L.	Nov 25 1941	Jan 7 1949	Jul 28 1954
144	Sheitz	W. E.	Nov 28 1941	Jan 8 1949	Jul 29 1954
145	Gillis	C. J.	Dec 1 1941	Jan 9 1949	
146	Cavellior	R. H.	Mar 25 1942	Jan 10 1949	Jul 30 1954
147	Sawyer	E. F.	Apr 25 1942	Jan 12 1949	
148	Dorgan	R. W.	May 4 1942	Jan 13 1949	Jul 31 1954
149	Legault	L. J.	May 4 1942	Feb 15 1952	Aug 10 1954
150	Greene	J. L.	May 18 1942	Jan 14 1949	Aug 1 1954
151	Whinfield	P. A.	May 30 1942		
152	Horth	R. V.	Jun 13 1942	Jan 15 1949	Aug 2 1954
153	Bowman	J. E.	Jun 20 1942	Jan 16 1949	Aug 3 1954
154	Stark	W. E.	Jul 4 1942	Jan 17 1949	Aug 4 1954

155	Lake	W. J.	Jul 10 1942	Jan 18 1949	Aug 5 1954
156	Stott	C. H.	Aug 1 1942	Jan 20 1949	
157	Trotter	F. V.	Aug 1 1942	Jan 21 1949	Aug 6 1954
158	Cardinal	V. D.	Aug 2 1942	Jan 22 1949	Aug 7 1954
159	Clark	D. W.	Aug 17 1942	Feb 16 1952	
160	Spencer	R. G.	Aug 18 1942	Jan 21 1949	Aug 8 1954
161	Cummings	R. F.	Aug 18 1942	Feb 17 1952	Aug 11 1954
162	Morris	G. E.	Aug 22 1942	Feb 18 1952	
163	Myers	J. W.	Aug 23 1942	Feb 19 1952	
164	Rusaw	R. C.	Sep 6 1942	Feb 20 1952	
165	Bellaradino	A.	Sep 23 1942		
166	Pierce	G. L.	Oct 19 1942	Feb 22 1952	
167	McDonald	L .W.	Oct 25 1942	Feb 23 1952	
168	Gagnon	H. L.	Oct 28 1942	Feb 24 1952	
169	Batchelor	D. R.	Oct 29 1942		
170	Fraser	M. J. Jr.	Nov 16 1942	Feb 25 1952	
171	Wicks	W. H.	Nov 16 1942	Feb 26 1952	
172	Bush	D. J.	Nov 16 1942	Feb 27 1952	
173	Perry	R. A.	Nov 21 1942	Feb 28 1952	
174	Marino	W. A.	Dec 25 1942	Feb 29 1952	
175	Vickery	V. E.	Feb 12 1943		
176	Lassail	H. E.	Mar 15 1943	Mar 2 1952	
177	Osborne	R. C.	Mar 17 1943	Jul 19 1954	
178	Bowman	C. E.	Mar 29 1943	Mar 3 1952	
179	Peters	E. W.	Mar 30 1943		
180	Currier	W. H.	Jul 22 1943	Jul 20 1954	
181	Bush	W. S.	Jul 29 1943		
182	Larocque	M. J.	Jul 31 1943	Jul 21 1954	
183	Benik	F. D. Jr.	Aug 18 1943	Jul 22 1954	
184	Clancy	J. F.	Nov 1 1943	Jul 23 1954	
185	Smith	C. C.	Nov 11 1943		
186	Doyle	B. J.	Dec 12 1943	Jul 24 1954	
187	Haggett	R. R.	Jan 3 1944		
188	Timmerman	F. D.	Jan 14 1944		
189	Ravas	J.	Apr 14 1944	Jul 25 1954	
190	Downing	H. S.	Apr 28 1944	Jul 26 1954	
191	Pollard	J. W.	Jul 15 1944	Jul 27 1954	
192	Storin	V. L.	Jul 22 1944		
193	Barry	E. N.	Sep 3 1944	Jul 28 1954	
194	Bailey	F. H.	Sep 10 1944		
195	Regan	J. J.	Oct 20 1944	Jul 29 1954	
196	Lavine	J. H.	Nov 24 1944		
197	Rico	A.	Apr 11 1945		
198	Horning	J. J.	May 28 1945	Jul 30 1954	
199	Brooks	W. T.	Jun 15 1945		
200	O'Leary	R. J.	Aug 7 1945		
201	Brady	C. F.	Sep 25 1945	Jul 31 1954	
202	Nieczkoski	C. J.	Sep 27 1945	Aug 1 1954	
203	Chateau	K.	Sep 29 1945		
204	Tyska	F. W.	Oct 2 1945	Aug 2 1954	
205	Delaney	G. A.	Dec 3 1945	Aug 3 1954	
206	Stillman	D. J.	Dec 6 1945		
207	Tyler	M. C.	Dec 12 1945		
208	Kaine	J. A. Jr.	Dec 12 1945		
209	Furney	F. A.	Jan 6 1946		

210	Bourgourd	R. C.	Jan 8 1946	
211	James	W. I.	Jan 17 1946	Aug 4 1954
212	Watkins	V. A.	Jan 18 1946	
213	Dylis	F. D.	Sep 1 1946	Aug 5 1954
214	Rogers	N. J.	Feb 27 1947	
215	Olson	R. W.	Feb 16 1947	Aug 6 1954
216	Tardge	E. J. Jr.	Mar 12 1947	
217	Hough	L. A.	Apr 10 1947	
218	Sullivan	A. F.	Apr 17 1947	
219	Marsh	R. M.	Jun 25 1947	
220	McHugh	R. E.	Aug 8 1947	
221	Cocco	R. H.	Sep 6 1947	
222	Gable	H. H.	Sep 6 1947	
223	Thomas	L. R.	Sep 9 1947	
224	Wright	F. R.	Oct 29 1947	
225	Cruze	C. C.	Nov 14 1947	Aug 7 1954
226	Doubles	J. H.	Nov 19 1947	
227	Girard	C. J.	Nov 24 1947	
228	Hanlon	R. B.	Jan 10 1948	
229	Petrie	E. L.	Jan 16 1948	
230 #	Emrich	G.	Feb 2 1948	
231	Merkley	L. H.	Feb 3 1948	
232	Duke	W. A.	Mar 25 1948	
233	Washburn	E. J.	Sep 2 1948	
234	Thackston	J. B.	Sep 29 1948	
235	Donoghue	L. F.	Oct 5 1950	
236	Mackey	L. B.	Oct 17 1950	Aug 8 1954
237	Duda	P. P. Sr.	Oct 18 1950	
238	Russell	R. J.	Oct 20 1950	
239	McCaffrey	R. S.	Oct 31 1950	
240	Marlenga	H. J.	Nov 1 1950	
241	Kennedy	R. S.	Nov 7 1950	
242	Latham	R. J.	Nov 10 1950	
243	Huntley	C. H.	Nov 10 1950	
244	Boehlert	R. K.	Jul 24 1951	
245	Bowman	J. E. Jr.	Jun 26 1954	
246	Brown	A. G.	Jun 26 1954	
247	Cardinal	D. J.	Jul 4 1954	
248	O'Leary	D. L.	Jul 22 1954	
249	Zimmer	G. H.	Oct 14 1954	

Seniority Dates of Yard Crews
January 1 1955

DP - Disability Pension # - Military Service

			Switchtender	Brakeman	Conductor
1	Morrison	E. J.			Dec 30 1907
2	Putnam	M. H.	Dec 7 1909	Sep 16 1911	
3	Gregory	G. H.	Dec 30 1910		Sep 17 1911
4	Meylor	J. P.	Jan 11 1911		Nov 27 1911
5	Sharlow	J.	Jul 29 1912		Aug 8 1912
6 DP	Clarke	D. G.			May 26 1916
7	Dibble	F. O.	Jun 15 1916		Jun 17 1916
8	Clarke	F. J.	Jun 16 1916		Jul 5 1916
9	Stansbury	W. J.	Jan 1 1917		Mar 12 1917
10	Walrath	E. D. Sr.			Mar 16 1917
11	Forshaw	M. J.	Sep 28 1916		Mar 21 1917
12	Boulia	A. J.			Apr 1 1917
13	Jareo	M. J.	Jul 17 1917	Apr 1 1917	
14	Topping	I. B.	Apr 4 1917		May 8 1917
15	Abell	S. C.			Jul 6 1917
16	O'Connor	J. D.	Jul 1 1918		
17	Carpenter	M. W.			Nov 14 1918
18	Michaels	W. J.	Jan 8 1919		Aug 4 1919
19	Richards	E. G.			Feb 5 1919
20	Quackenbush	W. W.			Feb 12 1920
21	Wilson	M.	Jul 5 1920		Dec 1 1920
22	Dawson	D. F.	Sep 20 1920		Dec 3 1920
23	Evans	R. C.	Dec 19 1926		Jan 14 1940
24 DP	Watson	J. E.	Dec 24 1925	Aug 14 1940	
25	Tapley	C. P.	Aug 29 1929		
26	Cronk	E. P.	Sep 5 1929		Jan 31 1941
27	English	W. F.	Dec 15 1940		Feb 1 1941
28	Williams	C. E.	Dec 22 1940		Feb 2 1941
29	Jareo	M. J. Jr.	Feb 1 1941		Mar 30 1941
30	Verbeck	L. E.	Jun 30 1941		Jul 26 1941
31	Hamel	K. R.	Jul 18 1941		Aug 29 1941
32 #	Newtown	M. A.	Aug 11 1941	Sep 1 1941	Jan 28 1946
33	Robare	R. E.	Aug 17 1941		Sep 10 1941
34	Woods	F. L.	Aug 29 1941		Sep 18 1941
35	Potter	R. D.	Aug 31 1941		Oct 17 1941
36	Podvin	G. F.	Sep 10 1941		Oct 23 1941
37	Wilson	F. E.	Oct 17 1941	Nov 17 1941	Jan 28 1946
38	Fowler	D. R.	Oct 19 1941		Nov 22 1941
39	Banville	A. J.	Nov 22 1941		Jul 11 1942
40	Priest	R. E.	Dec 19 1941	Jul 30 1942	
41	McMillan	R. F.	Mar 15 1942		
42	O'Connor	C. H.	Jul 26 1942		Dec 2 1942
43	George	H. F.	Aug 31 1942		Dec 3 1942
44	Sprague	R. L.	Feb 27 1943		Mar 23 1943

45	Avery	H. O.	Mar 20 1943		Apr 4 1943
46	Anderson	M. B.	Mar 22 1943		Sep 5 1943
47	Buszak	S. S.	Oct 10 1943		Nov 24 1943
48 #	Lawyer	E. F.	Dec 16 1943	Jan 18 1944	
49	Chartier	J. C.	Jan 16 1944	May 1 1944	
50	Maher	L.	Mar 1 1944		Mar 1 1944
51	Frederick	E. J.	May 10 1944	May 10 1944	Jan 28 1946
52	Smith	R.	Mar 14 1944	May 14 1944	Jan 28 1946
53	Touron	C. O.	Jan 13 1945	Jan 13 1945	
54	Cummings	H. R.	Mar 27 1945	Mar 27 1945	
55	Barry	W. J.	Apr 13 1945		Apr 13 1945
56	Ogden	A. C.	Jul 29 1945		Jul 29 1945
57	Wells	K. E.	Aug 20 1945		Aug 20 1945
58	Fagan	J. A.	Nov 28 1945	Nov 28 1945	
59	Kellogg	D. J.	Dec 6 1945		Dec 6 1945
60	Washburn	K. G.	Dec 10 1945		Dec 10 1945
61	Bijory	C. S.	Dec 11 1945		Dec 11 1945
62	Payne	J. L.	Dec 29 1945		Dec 29 1945
63	Spradlin	V. H.	Nov 1 1946	Nov 1 1946	
64	LaJuette	R. F.	Feb 1 1947	Feb 1 1947	
65	Caputo	A. J.	Feb 2 1947		
66	LaJuette	H. C.	Feb 9 1947	Feb 9 1947	
67	Clarke	F. P.	Mar 19 1947	Jan 6 1948	
68	Hanlon	R. B.	Jan 10 1948	Mar 15 1948	
69 #	Emrich	G.	Feb 2 1948	Feb 2 1948	
70	Washburn	E. J.	Sep 2 1948	Sep 2 1948	
71	Thackston	J. B.	Sep 29 1948	Oct 4 1950	
72	Huntley	C. H.	Nov 10 1950	Nov 10 1950	
			Oswego		**Conductor**
73	Rehor	G. F.			Apr 3 1916